ASP.NET
Web Services

By

Yashavant Kanetkar
Asang Dani

BPB PUBLICATIONS
B-14, CONNAUGHT PLACE, NEW DELHI-1

FIRST EDITION 2009

Copyright © BPB Publications, INDIA.

ISBN –10: 81-8333-279-X / 13: 978-81-8333-279-8

All Right Reserved. No part of this publication may be reproduced or distributed in any form or by any means or stored in a database or retrieval system, without the prior written permission of publisher, with the exception that the program listings may be entered, stored and executed in a computer system, but they may not be reproduced for publication.

LIMITS OF LIABILITY AND DISCLAIMER OF WARRANTY

The information contained in this book is to the best of the author's knowledge true and correct. The author has made every effort to ensure accuracy of this publications, but cannot be held responsible for any loss or damage arising from any information in this book.

All trademarks referred to in the book are acknowledged as properties of their respective owners.

Distributors:

COMPUTER BOOK CENTRE
12, Shrungar Shopping Centre, M.G. Road,
BANGALORE-560001 Ph: 25587923, 25584641

MICRO BOOKS
Shanti Niketan Building, 8, Camac Street
KOLKATTA-700017 Ph: 22826518/9

24756967
BUSINESS PROMOTION BUREAU
8/1, Ritchie Street, Mount Road,
CHENNAI-600002 Ph: 28410796, 2855049 I

BPB PUBLICATIONS
B-14, Connaught Place, NEW DELHI-110001
Ph : 23325760, 23723393, 23737742

BPB BOOK CENTRE
376, Old Lajpat Rai Market, DELHI-110006
Ph: 23861747

MICRO MEDIA
Shop No Chambers, 150 D.N. Rd,.5,Mahendra
Next to Capital Cinema V.T. (C.S.T.) Station,
MUMBAI-400001 Ph: 22078296, 22078297

DECCAN AGENCIES
4-3-329, Bank Street,
HYDERABAD-500195 Ph: 24756400,

INTO TECH
G-2, Sidhartha Building , 96, Nehru Place,
NEW DELHI-110019
Ph: 26438245, 26415092, 26234208

INFO TECH
Shop No. 2, F-38, South Extention Part-I
NEW DELHI-110049
Ph: 24691288

Published by **Munish Jain** for BPB Publications, B-14, Connaught Place, New Delhi-110001 and Printed by him at Akash Press New Delhi.

Dedicated to
Prabhakar Kanetkar

- *Yashavant Kanetkar*

Dedicated to
Neelima and Kamalakar Dani

- *Asang Dani*

About the Authors

Yashavant Kanetkar

Through his original works in the form of books and Quest Video Courseware CDs Yashavant has created, moulded and groomed lacs of IT careers in the last decade and half. In recognition of his contribution he has been awarded the "Best .NET Technical Contributor" and "Most Valuable Professional" awards by Microsoft. Yashavant holds a BE from VJTI Mumbai and M.Tech. from IIT Kanpur. Yashavant's current affiliations include being a Director of KICIT and KSET.

Asang Dani

Asang holds a BE in Electronics Engineering from VRCE, Nagpur and ME in Computer Science from IISc, Bangalore. Asang has a rich Real-time Embedded Systems and Storage Networking experience that he obtained while working for companies like Veritas, Microsoft and Dow Jones. Asang's current areas of interest include .NET Technologies, Window CE, Device Drivers and Embedded Linux. Asang is currently Director of KICIT and KSET.

Yashavant's and Asang's current activities can be tracked at http://quest.ksetindia.com/

Acknowledgments

Building Web Services is relatively easy as compared to understanding and appreciating the rationale behind them. It took us some time to digest this rationale. Once we did that we found them extremely appealing. In the process we were required to dig and unearth lots of articles and books and seek online converstations with many software practitioners. This list is long and we would like to thank all of them.

In spite of all the digital tools available at our disposal, book writing still remains a laborious process. Monali eased this process to a great extent through her thoroughness in every aspect of compilation of this book.

Jayant has been instrumental in convincing that the novel cover design of this book would be more appealing to the readers rather than the graphics that we have been using for other titles. Many thanks to him for this new idea.

Finally, we would like to thank our families for supporting us in ways that are beyond our ability of constructing words for them.

Yashavant Kanetkar
Asang Dani

Contents

	Introduction	
1.	At Your Majesty's Service	1
2.	Consume It Your Majesty	7
3.	Web Services Under The Hood	19
4.	Asynchronous Web Services Client	25
5.	Creating Currency Web Service	35
6.	Nuances Of Web Services	45
7.	Show Me The Money!	53
8.	Nobody Is Perfect!	61
9.	Until We REST!	69
10.	Finally, Some REST!	87
	Appendix A	99

Introduction

World wide web is all about diversity. Millions of computing devices using different microprocessors, different Operating Systems, different network technologies running applications built using different technologies and languages wish to communicate with one another in a meaningful manner. So today's truly global application is in true sense of the word a distributed application where different pieces of the same application are physically running on different systems and might be built using different languages and technologies. To facilitate communication between these truly distributed applications it is necessary to create software services that are powerful and reusable and yet simple to use. In the past, the software world has tried to address this scenario by evolving technologies like CORBA and COM. These have met with varying degrees of success. Some of these technologies were difficult to use and were tied to specific computing platforms whereas, others lacked the marketing muscle and the appeal to make them succesful in a global marketplace. Web Services seems to be a perfect choice for providing distributed computing services in this scenario. They are elegant and powerful and addresses all the concerns mentioned above.

This book is about building practical Web Services using the .NET platform. These Web Services can be used from a .NET application or a Java application from a PC/Laptop or from a mobile device.

The best way to master a technology is to use it in creating something meaningful, something which is non-trivial. That way the chances are good that you will get to know and use most of the aspects of the technology that you are trying to learn. Towards this end we decided to create a content delivery platform called "Quest". As expected, while creating this we came across numerous situations where there were trade-offs in deciding which feature of the .NET technology to use to carry out the implementation of the task at hand. We also landed ourselves into several questions for which there were no straight answers. But as we proceeded we started documenting all that we were learning. At the end we are a satisfied lot—because not only the Quest Content Delivery platform that we created using .NET being used in the market to disseminate several courses on programming languages and technologies; in addition we also have a book which you are holding right now that contains answers to all the questions that we came across while carrying our the development of Quest.

That is how we learnt the nuances of Web Services. We urge you to follow in the same footsteps and try to create some meaning Web Service once you are through with the book. This way you would get a good insight into development of Web Services. All the best!

Needless to say we are willing to hear all that you have to say about this edition and more. We are available at kanetkar@ksetindia.com and asang@ksetindia.com.

Yashavant Kanetkar
Asang Dani

1

At Your Majesty's Service

C programming language was instrumental in taking the art of programming to masses. More than 35 years later, Web Services are transforming the way we do programming, in an equally, if not more, dramatic manner. Procedural programming gave rise to Object Oriented Programming. With the spread of TCP/IP networking, Web Services now enable you to build software in truly distributed and reusable manner. In short, they represent libraries on the network. In this journey, we will show you how the web allows companies and individuals as diverse as people on this planet to create software for the coming decades.

Evolution of Web Services

Till early 1970's, programming was being practiced only in the best of the academic institutions. Access to computers, operating systems, editors, compilers and associated tools was a big issue. In 1980's and 90's Berkeley's BSD and AT&T's Unix operating system enabled people to develop wide variety of software. As software became more complex, need to build reusable software was felt. To meet this need, Static and dynamic libraries were created in various areas. C library more affectionately known as "libc" served as a guiding force to programmers in designing the so called "function libraries". Power of abstraction was first felt by programmers at large in a major way. They stretched their own limits to create more powerful software and applications. Complexity in modern software finally led to adoption of Object Oriented Programming principles in building software. Languages like (initially) Ada and (later) C++ allowed creation of truly reusable software components using principles like encapsulation, polymorphism, inheritance, containership etc. These components were bundled into reusable libraries like Microsoft's MFC (Microsoft Foundation Classes), Borland OWL (Object Window Library) etc.

As the technology became more mature, and it was widely used in various large organizations, diversity of computing platforms became a big issue. Portability, compatibility, upgradeability, data exchange formats etc. became catchwords as Software/applications from different sources/companies refused to gel cohesively. This is when need for truly "standardized" distributed computing was felt. IETF (Internet Engineering and Task Force) standardized RPC – Remote Procedure Call in 1988. It allowed programs on two different systems to communicate using APIs that took parameters and returned values. NFS (Network File System) implementation on various flavors of UNIX embraced this approach. In the last decade of 20th century, several new programming languages like Java, Python, Ruby, C#, VB.NET were created and gained widespread acceptance. It was clear that new approach to distributed computing was required. This approach had to be:

Chapter 1: At Your Majesty's Service   3

(a)   Language neutral
(b)   Easy to implement on server
(c)   Easy to use on client

Various approaches were tried including COM/DCOM, CORBA. Though both these approaches let people communicate between client and server in a language neutral way, they were pretty complex to use. With the advent of Web Services, all these problems got solved satisfactorily. In the next section we will discuss the web services approach to distributed computing in detail. We are sure that your fingers must be itching to create your very own web service. In our opinion, to be able to create one good thing, you must first see ten good things. This applies to web services as well. Hence, we will see how to use a web service, and subsequently migrate to creating a web service. But even before we learn how to use a web service, we must understand how a Web Service works.

How A Web Service Works

A web service is always deployed on a server. Once deployed, it can be accessed through one or more clients simultaneously. A web service can be written in one programming language and can be accessed through any other programming language. For example, a Currency Conversion Web Service written in C# can easily be accessed by a Java client. Suppose, the currency conversion web service has following functions:

Function	Description
CountryCurrency GetCurrency (String cname)	Returns the currency details for specified country
float GetRateByCountry (String from, String to)	Returns the latest rate of conversion from one country's currency to another
float GetRateBySymbol (String from, String to)	Returns the latest rate of conversion from one currency symbol to another
String [ ] GetCountryNames()	Returns an array of country names
CountryCurrency [ ] GetCountryCurrencies()	Returns an array containing names of all countries along with their currency names and symbols

Figure 1.1 Functions in Currency web service

Using the currency conversion web service involves making calls to these functions. Only difference being these calls will happen over the network. To facilitate these remote calls coming from clients written in different languages running on different platforms there is need for a standard method:

(a)   To specify which method is being called
(b)   To pass arguments to this method

This seemingly simple job is much more complex because:

(a)   Sizes of data types are different across languages.
(b)   String representation might be in ASCII in one language in Unicode in other.
(c)   Some platforms may use a big-endian byte-order, whereas others may use little-endian byte-order.
(d)   Internal representation of objects that may be passed to functions is different in different languages.

Hence a standard called SOAP (Simple Object Access Protocol) was evolved. It addresses the above issues in the following manner:

(a)   All basic data types are converted to strings before passing them remotely.
(b)   All strings are converted to Unicode string before passing them.
(c)   Since SOAP converts every data type to a string, endianness doesn't matter (endianness affects only numbers).
(d)   Objects are serialized suitably before passing them over network.

When we call a function in a web service, the call is first converted into a SOAP message envelope. This SOAP message envelope is represented in the form of XML and sent to the server as a request using the most commonly used network transfer protocol, namely HTTP. When the web service function returns a value it is again converted into a SOAP message envelope and returned as a HTTP response.

The process of converting a function call into a SOAP envelope is called serialization, whereas, converting the SOAP envelope back into language-specific data types is called deserialization. Note that the job of serialization on client, sending HTTP request from the client, deserialization on server, serialization of return value on the server, sending HTTP response and deserializing the return value on the client is not to be done by us. It is done by a proxy class on the client side and a web service class on the server side. Note that the proxy class is created by the client framework (Visual

Sudio 2005 if the client is written in C# or VB.NET and by NetBeans 5.5/6.0 if the client is written in Java). The details of the proxy class creation would be discussed when we show you how to create the web service client. The essence of working of a web service is captured in the following figure.

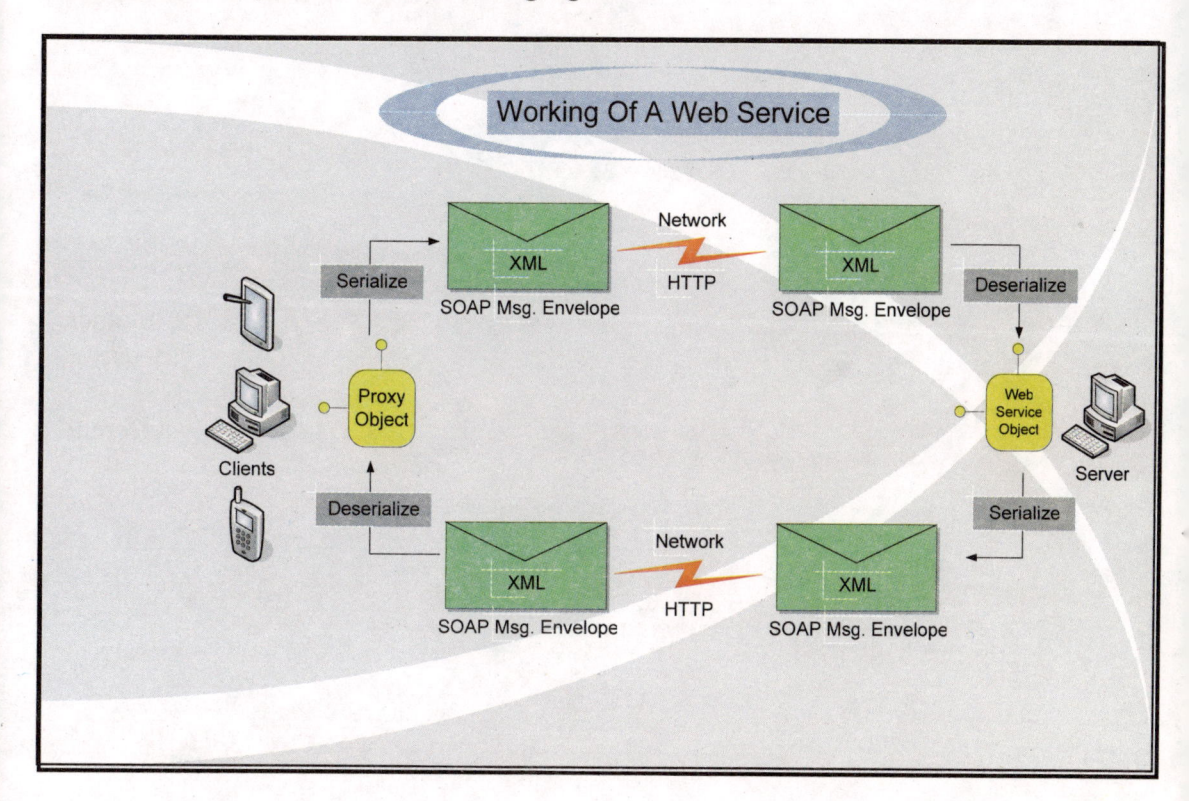

Figure 1.1 – Working of a web service

We hope that by now you have a clear idea about what web services are all about. In the next chapter we will see how to use the currency converter web service through a client program.

Chapter 2: Consume It, Your Majesty

2

Consume it, Your Majesty

ASP.Net Web Services

Paid or free, small or big, secure or insecure, scalable or otherwise, .NET based or Java based …. all web services serve one single minded purpose… letting the viewer, look at the world. They throw open a world, which is yours for the taking, we are sure that by the time you reach end of this series, you would get more than a glimpse of their power and utility.

Getting Ready to use a Web Service

To use web services through .NET platform, we need one of the following tools:

- Visual Studio 2005 Professional
- Visual Studio 2005 Express Editions (C# or VB.NET)

Once we have one of these tools on our system, we can start exploring the web services right away. First question that comes to mind is - where is the web service that I wish to use, located? Well, where else but on the network. To be able to access a web service, we must either know the URL where it is located or we must be able to discover it. As you can guess, the first method is simpler. Hence, for this chapter we would use the first way.

We have created one such web service called **CurrencyService**. It is located at:

http://quest.ksetindia.com/services/CurrencyService/

Open your web browser and type this URL in the address bar. On doing so, the following output will appear.

Chapter 2: Consume It, Your Majesty

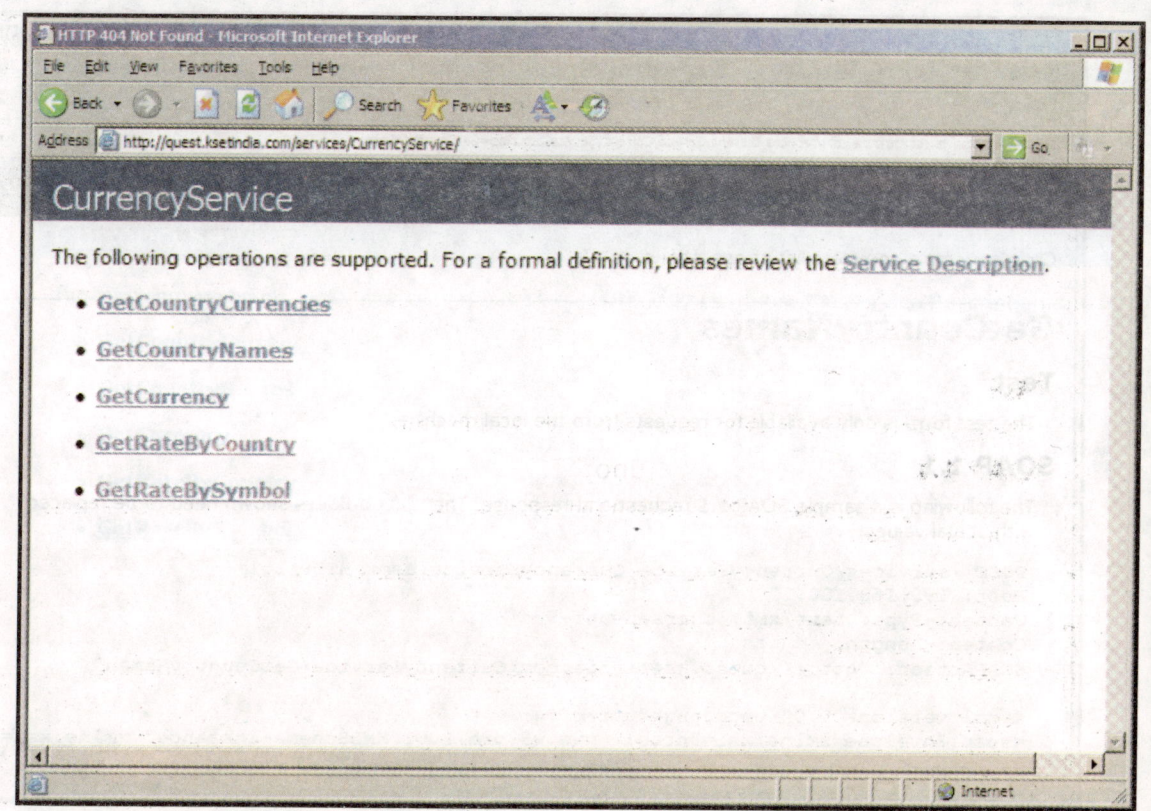

Figure 2.1 – Locating a web service

At the outset, we are shown a list of supported operations also called as APIs (Application Programmer's Interfaces). Clicking on any of the operations like *GetCountryNames*, shows the following output:

ASP.Net Web Services

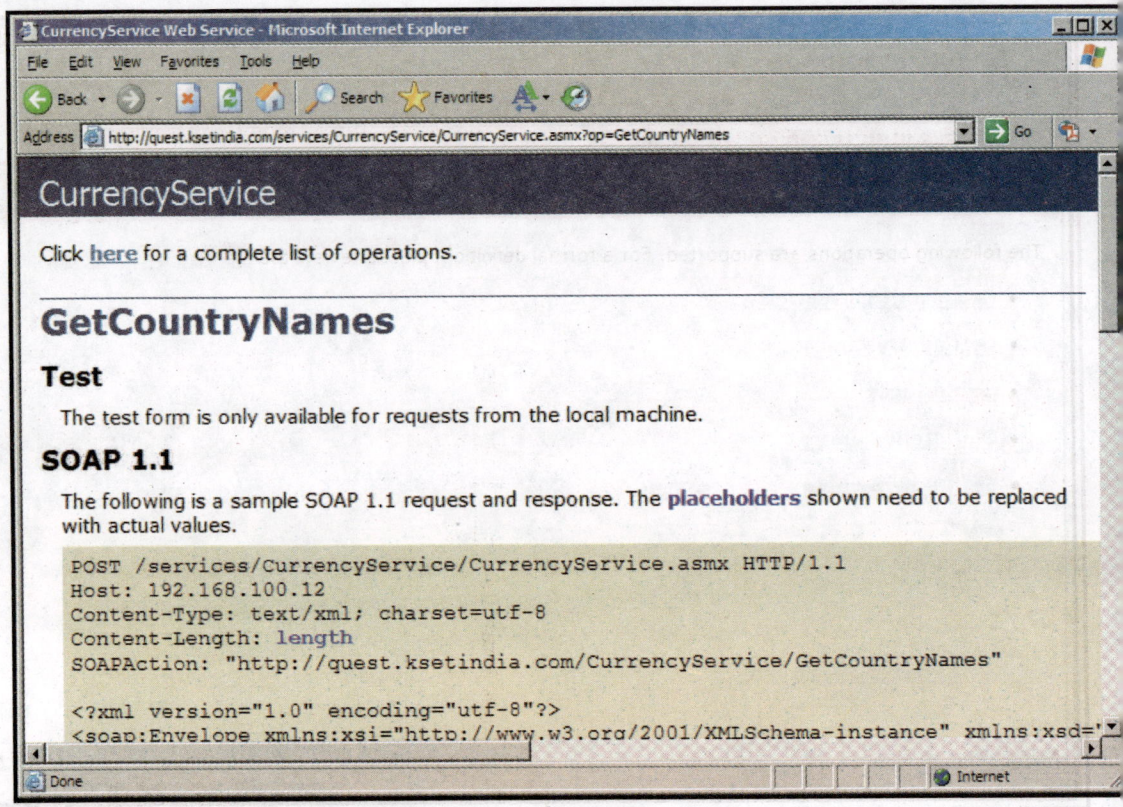

Figure 2.2 – Exploring Operations in a web service

By now you must be wondering - "is this is how we use a web service?" Answer is a definite no. This simply gives you some idea about the web service. It is not enough to start using the web service in our program. To use the web service in our program, we need its description in XML format. This description is as per a standard called WSDL (Web Service Description Language). Easiest way to get this description is to click on "Service Description" link given on the front-page of **CurrencyService**. When you click on this link, it produces following output.

Chapter 2: Consume It, Your Majesty   **11**

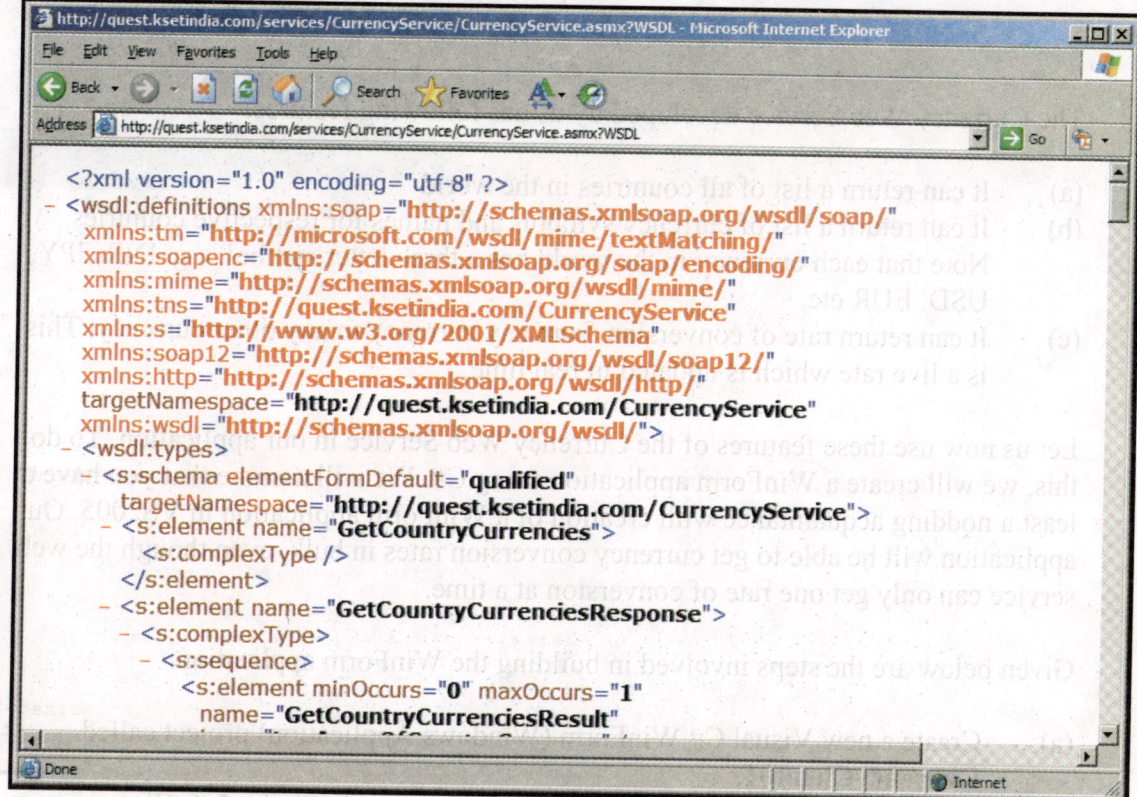

```
<?xml version="1.0" encoding="utf-8" ?>
- <wsdl:definitions xmlns:soap="http://schemas.xmlsoap.org/wsdl/soap/"
    xmlns:tm="http://microsoft.com/wsdl/mime/textMatching/"
    xmlns:soapenc="http://schemas.xmlsoap.org/soap/encoding/"
    xmlns:mime="http://schemas.xmlsoap.org/wsdl/mime/"
    xmlns:tns="http://quest.ksetindia.com/CurrencyService"
    xmlns:s="http://www.w3.org/2001/XMLSchema"
    xmlns:soap12="http://schemas.xmlsoap.org/wsdl/soap12/"
    xmlns:http="http://schemas.xmlsoap.org/wsdl/http/"
    targetNamespace="http://quest.ksetindia.com/CurrencyService"
    xmlns:wsdl="http://schemas.xmlsoap.org/wsdl/">
  - <wsdl:types>
    - <s:schema elementFormDefault="qualified"
        targetNamespace="http://quest.ksetindia.com/CurrencyService">
      - <s:element name="GetCountryCurrencies">
          <s:complexType />
        </s:element>
      - <s:element name="GetCountryCurrenciesResponse">
        - <s:complexType>
          - <s:sequence>
              <s:element minOccurs="0" maxOccurs="1"
                name="GetCountryCurrenciesResult"
```

Figure 2.3 – WSDL for CurrencyService web service

If you casually glance through the output, you will notice that it contains description of:

(a)   Each operation supported by the web service
(b)   Parameters for each operation
(c)   Return type if any

This is all that we need to know about WSDL! If you are interested, you can visit http://www.w3.org/TR/wsdl and soak yourself in the details of WSDL specification. In our opinion, this is not required just as yet. From now on, using **CurrencyWebService** mentioned above, would simply require you to refer to this URL:

http://quest.ksetindia.com/services/CurrencyService/CurrencyService.asmx?WSDL

Let us now create a simple WinForm application to access this web service.

Using the Currency Web Service

The Currency Web Service developed by us has following features:

(a)   It can return a list of all countries in the world
(b)   It can return a list of currency symbols and names for respective countries. Note that each currency in the world has a three letter symbol, e.g. INR, JPY, USD, EUR etc.
(c)   It can return rate of conversion from any currency to any other currency. This is a live rate which is updated in real time.

Let us now use these features of the Currency Web Service in our application. To do this, we will create a WinForm application using C#. We will assume that you have at least a nodding acquaintance with creation of a WinForm application in VS2005. Our application will be able to get currency conversion rates in bulk, even though the web service can only get one rate of conversion at a time.

Given below are the steps involved in building the WinForm application:

(a)   Create a new Visual C# WinForm (Windows Application) project called **CurrencyClient01**.
(b)   Drag and drop controls on the WinForm as shown in Figure 2.4. Give names to the controls as indicated in the figure.

Chapter 2: Consume It, Your Majesty   13

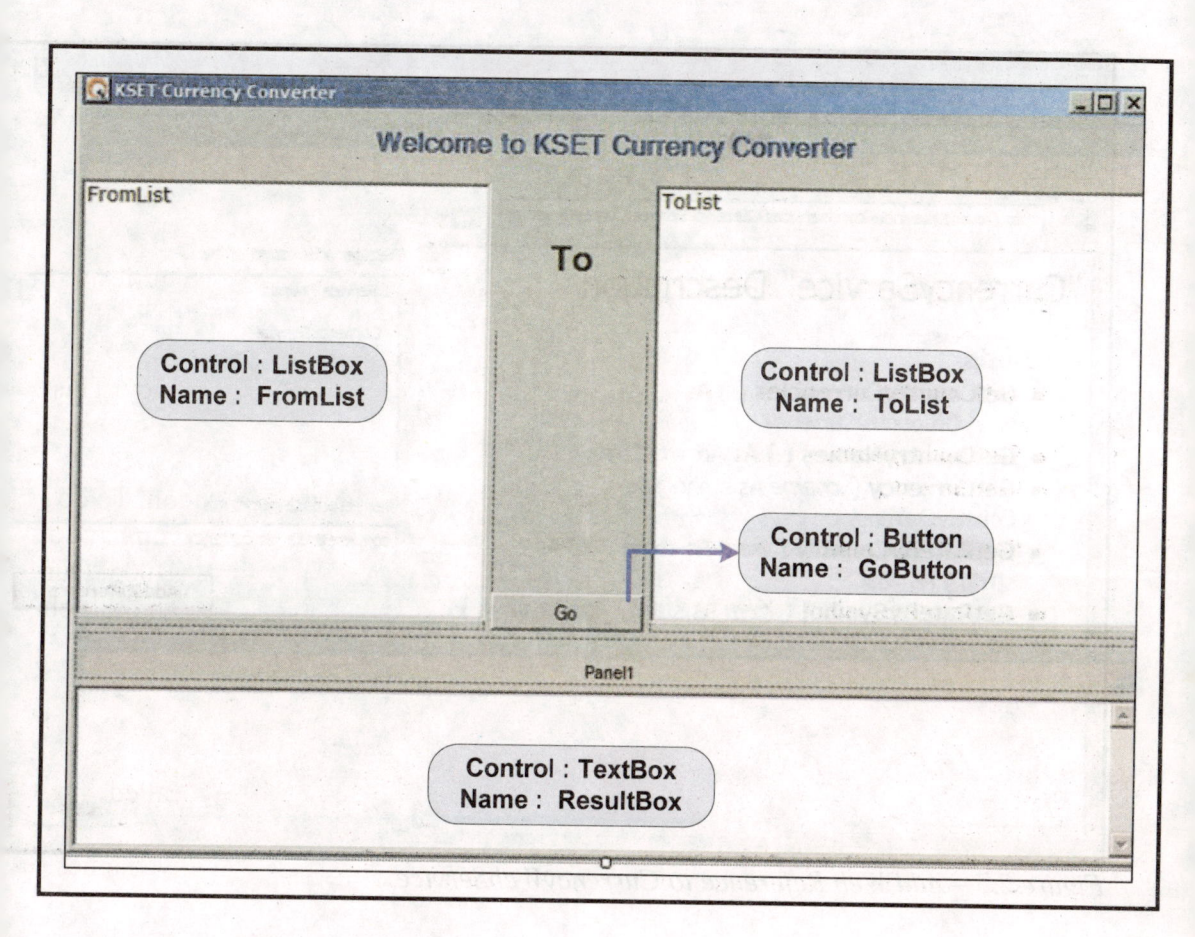

Figure 2.4 – WinForm Controls

(c)   Add *Web Reference* to the *CurrenyWebService* from Solution explorer window by right clicking on *References* node. When prompted to enter the reference name, add **com.ksetindia.ws.currency** as shown in Figure 2.5.

ASP.Net Web Services

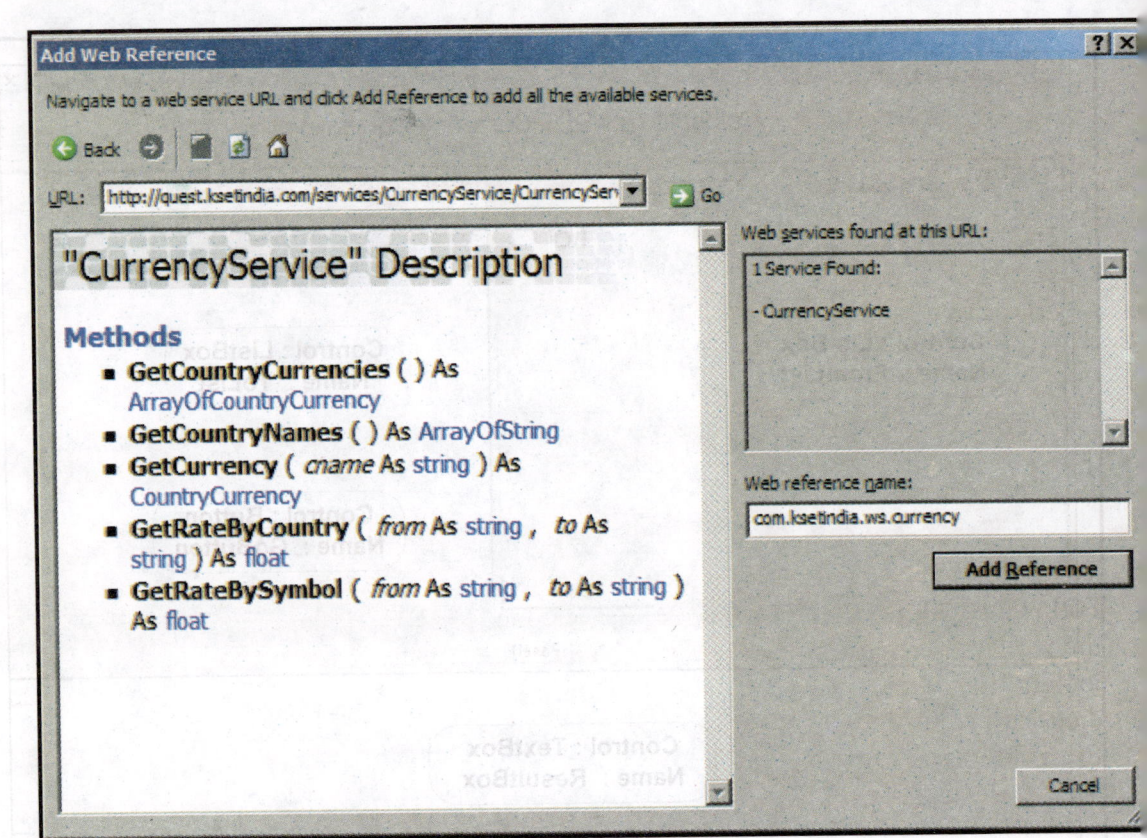

Figure 2.5 – Add Web Reference to CurrencyWebService

Visual Studio creates a proxy class called **CurrencyWebService** on your machine. It communicates with the web service. The class is automatically placed inside the namespace **CurrencyClient01.com.ksetindia.ws.currency**. We have to add the following statement at the top of **CurrencyClient.cs** to be able to use the proxy class.

```
using CurrencyClient01.com.ksetindia.ws.currency ;
```

(d)   Add event handlers **CurrencyClient_Load( )** and **GoButton_Click( )** to CurrencyClient.cs.

Before we get into the event handlers, we need to do some initialization work in the constructor. This is shown below:

Chapter 2: Consume It, Your Majesty 15

```
private CurrencyService service ;
private SortedDictionary<String, CountryCurrency> countries ;

public CurrencyClient( )
{
   InitializeComponent( ) ;
   service = new CurrencyService( ) ;
   countries = new SortedDictionary<string,CountryCurrency>( );
   foreach( CountryCurrency c in
        service.GetCountryCurrencies( ) )
      countries.Add ( c.country, c ) ;
}
```

To use the web service, we must create an object of the proxy class **CurrencyService**. Following this, we have obtained the list of counties and their currencies by calling the web service function **GetCountryCurrencies( )** using the object **service**. For easy lookup from country name to its currency and symbol, we have created a sorted dictionary with county name as the key and **CountryCurrency** object as the value. Each **CountryCurrency** object holds country name, currency and its symbol.

Event Handlers

Let us now look at the code that you need to you need to add for the event handlers. In the Form load event handler, we populate the two listboxes with the names of the countries retrieved from the web service by calling **GetCountryNames( )**. This is shown below.

```
private void CurrencyClient_Load ( object sender,
                                   EventArgs e )
{
   FromList.DataSource = service.GetCountryNames( ) ;
   ToList.DataSource = service.GetCountryNames( ) ;
}
```

When the user selects, the source and target country names, and clicks on the **Go** button, the **doConversion( )** function is called by the **Go** button's click handler.

```
private void GoButton_Click ( object sender, EventArgs e )
{
  doConversion( ) ;
}
```

In the **doConversion( )** function, we walk through the list of source and target countries one by one and get their conversion rates using their respective currency symbols. **GetRateBySymbol( )** web service function is used for this purpose. This is shown below.

```
private void doConversion( )
{
  if ( FromList.SelectedItems.Count == 0 ||
       ToList.SelectedItems.Count == 0 )
    return ;

  ResultBox.Text = "" ;

  for ( int i = 0 ; i < FromList.SelectedItems.Count ; i++ )
  {
    string from = FromList.SelectedItems[ i ].ToString( ) ;
    CountryCurrency fromC = countries[ from ] ;

    for ( int j = 0 ; j < ToList.SelectedItems.Count ; j++ )
    {
      CountryCurrency toC ;
      toC = countries[ ToList.SelectedItems[ j ].ToString( )];
      ResultBox.Text +=
        String.Format ( "1 {0} {1} = {2} {3} {4}" +
                        Environment.NewLine,
          fromC.country, fromC.currency,
          service.GetRateBySymbol ( fromC.symbol, toC.symbol),
          toC.country, toC.currency ) ;
```

Chapter 2: Consume It, Your Majesty   17

```
      }
    }
}
```

If you select America and Australia from the source listbox and India and Japan from the target listbox, and click Go button, then the conversion rates would be displayed in the **ResultBox** as shown in Figure 2.6.

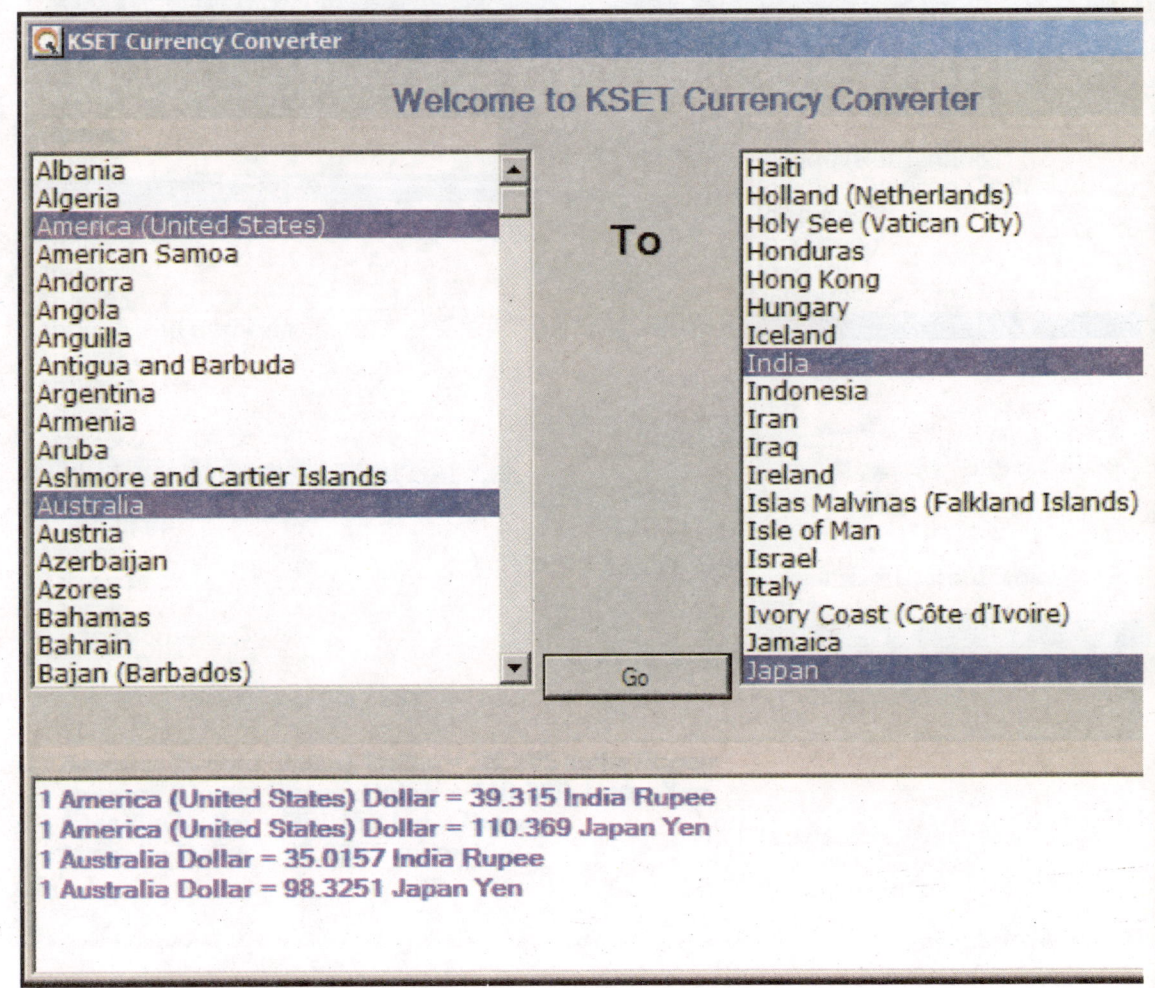

```
KSET Currency Converter
              Welcome to KSET Currency Converter

Albania                              Haiti
Algeria                              Holland (Netherlands)
America (United States)              Holy See (Vatican City)
American Samoa          To           Honduras
Andorra                              Hong Kong
Angola                               Hungary
Anguilla                             Iceland
Antigua and Barbuda                  India
Argentina                            Indonesia
Armenia                              Iran
Aruba                                Iraq
Ashmore and Cartier Islands          Ireland
Australia                            Islas Malvinas (Falkland Islands)
Austria                              Isle of Man
Azerbaijan                           Israel
Azores                               Italy
Bahamas                              Ivory Coast (Côte d'Ivoire)
Bahrain                              Jamaica
Bajan (Barbados)           Go        Japan

1 America (United States) Dollar = 39.315 India Rupee
1 America (United States) Dollar = 110.369 Japan Yen
1 Australia Dollar = 35.0157 India Rupee
1 Australia Dollar = 98.3251 Japan Yen
```

Figure 2.6 – Conversion rates for many to many

That brings us to the end of our first tryst with the web services. You would agree that with modern development tools like VS2005, building an application that consumes a

18   ASP.Net Web Services

web service is almost a child's play. Having said that, let us tell you that we have merely scratched the surface. Down below, there are very many issues that one needs to tackle while consuming web services. Do some of these issues occur to you? Think it over, or wait till the next chapter.

Chapter 3: Web Services Under The Hood   19

3

Web Services Under The Hood

In the last chapter, we had built a WinForm application to consume the **CurrencyWebService**. Though the application looked apparently simple, in our opinion, to fully fathom and utilize the power of web services it is necessary to take a peek at what happens under the hood when we are using web services. This is what we wish to do now.

Proxy class generation

We intend to cover a lot of ground here. Let us understand the implications of the steps that we carried out for consuming the **CurrencyWebService**. The three simple steps that we performed were as under:

(a)　Create a new Visual C# WinForm project and add controls to it.
(b)　Add *Web Reference* to the **CurrenyWebService**.
(c)　Add event handlers **CurrencyClient_Load( )** and **GoButton_Click( )**.

When we add the reference to the **CurrencyWebService**, VS2005 generates a lot of infrastructure code to facilitate the usage of this web service. Do realize that there is nothing magical about it. VS2005 simply invokes a utility called **wsdl.exe** for this purpose. If you wish you can also invoke this utility at command-line as shown below:

```
C:\> wsdl.exe /n:CurrencyClient02.com.ksetindia.ws.currency /l:cs /o:CurrencyService.cs
         http://localhost/CurrencyService/CurrencyService.asmx?WSDL
```

Let us now see the purpose of the command-line options that we have used. Their purpose is mentioned in the following table:

Option	Details
/n:CurrencyClient02.com.ksetindia.ws.currency	Namespace in which all the types created for this web service will be placed.
/l:cs	Language to use. In addition to C#, wsdl can generate code in VB.NET, J# or C++
/o:CurrencyService.cs	Name of the output file
http://localhost/CurrencyService/CurrencyService.asmx?WSDL	URL for the web service

Table 3.1 – wsdl.exe options

Chapter 3: Web Services Under The Hood

wsdl.exe generates a whole lot of code. Instead of getting bogged down in that code, let us understand the philosophy that it adopts. Once we grasp this philosophy, we can work with any other web service with equal ease. The essence of the code generated is captured in Figure 3.1 given below.

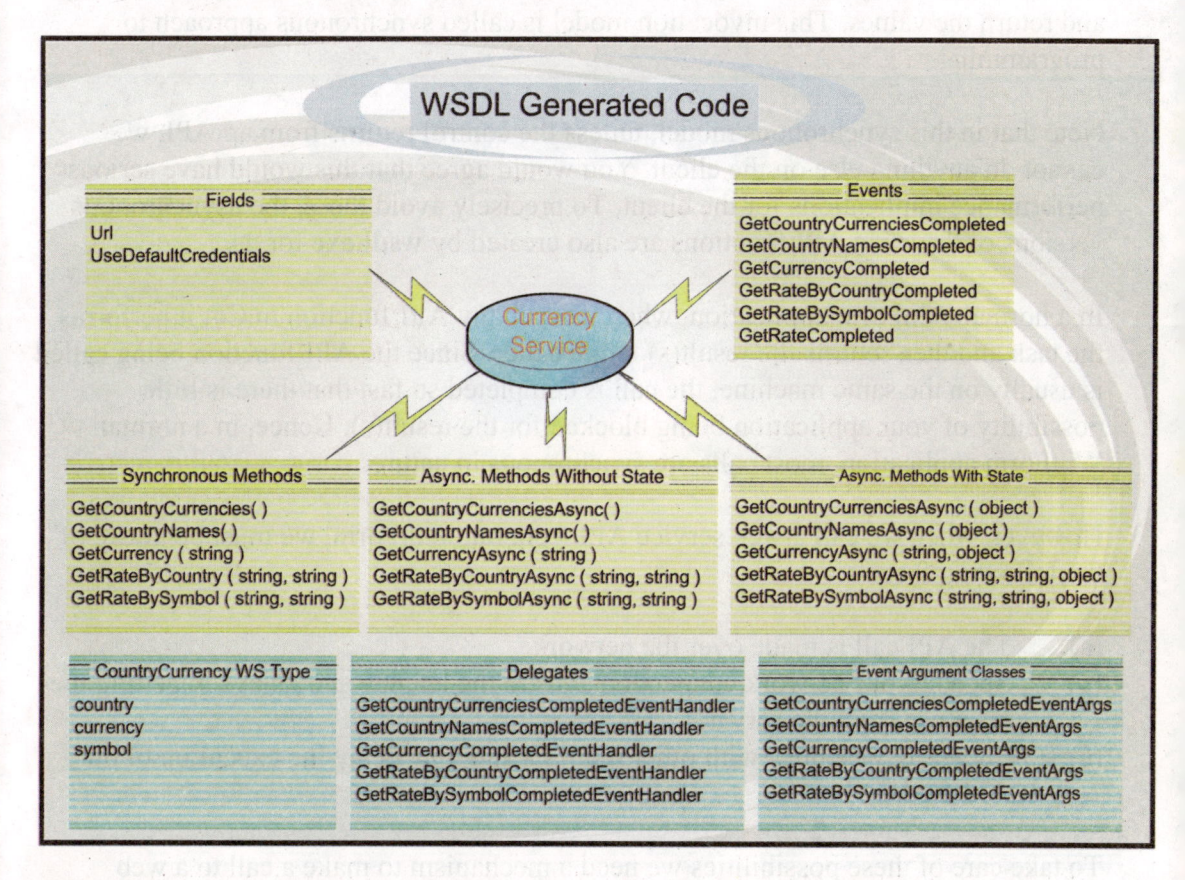

```
                          WSDL Generated Code

    ┌─── Fields ───┐                          ┌─── Events ───┐
    Url                                       GetCountryCurrenciesCompleted
    UseDefaultCredentials                     GetCountryNamesCompleted
                                              GetCurrencyCompleted
                                              GetRateByCountryCompleted
                          ( Currency          GetRateBySymbolCompleted
                            Service )         GetRateCompleted

    ┌─ Synchronous Methods ─┐  ┌─ Async. Methods Without State ─┐  ┌─ Async. Methods With State ─┐
    GetCountryCurrencies()     GetCountryCurrenciesAsync()         GetCountryCurrenciesAsync( object )
    GetCountryNames()          GetCountryNamesAsync()              GetCountryNamesAsync( object )
    GetCurrency( string )      GetCurrencyAsync( string )          GetCurrencyAsync( string, object )
    GetRateByCountry( string, string )  GetRateByCountryAsync( string, string )  GetRateByCountryAsync( string, string, object )
    GetRateBySymbol( string, string )   GetRateBySymbolAsync( string, string )   GetRateBySymbolAsync( string, string, object )

    ┌─ CountryCurrency WS Type ─┐  ┌─── Delegates ───┐               ┌─ Event Argument Classes ─┐
    country                        GetCountryCurrenciesCompletedEventHandler   GetCountryCurrenciesCompletedEventArgs
    currency                       GetCountryNamesCompletedEventHandler        GetCountryNamesCompletedEventArgs
    symbol                         GetCurrencyCompletedEventHandler            GetCurrencyCompletedEventArgs
                                   GetRateByCountryCompletedEventHandler       GetRateByCountryCompletedEventArgs
                                   GetRateBySymbolCompletedEventHandler        GetRateBySymbolCompletedEventArgs
```

Figure 3.1- Code generated by wsdl.exe

Understanding Generated Code

Let us now try to understand the purpose and meaning of the code generated by wsdl.exe. As shown in Figure 1(a), **CurrencyWebService** proxy class contains two kinds of APIs:

(a)   Synchronous
(b)   Asynchronous

This classification needs some explanation. In our Winform application, we used APIs like **GetCountryNames( )**, **GetCountryCurrencies( )** & **GetRateBySymbol()**. When we call them, they perform the task and return the result(s) to the caller. When we call them, it may take a long time for them to complete the execution (on server) and return the values. This invocation model is called synchronous approach to programming.

Note that in this synchronous model, unless the control returns from an API, we cannot do anything else on the client. You would agree that this would have serious performance implications for the client. To precisely avoid these, the asynchronous versions of the same API functions are also created by **wsdl.exe** for us.

In a normal WinForm application, when we call any API/function in C#, it performs the task and then returns the result(s) to the caller. Since the API/function being called is usually on the same machine, the call is completed so fast that there is little possibility of your application being blocked for the result(s). Hence, in a normal WinForm application, most calls are synchronous in nature.

However, when we call a web service API from our WinForm, we must be aware of the following facts:

(a) The API call is made over the network.
(b) Speed of our network connection adds to the latency and delays in getting the response from the server.
(c) Server may be busy with other requests and may delay the execution of our API further.

To take care of these possibilities we need a mechanism to make a call to a web service API and return immediately to do other work (without waiting for result(s) to become available). This is the purpose for which **wsdl.exe** creates the asynchronous versions of all the APIs in a web service. Thus, APIs in a web service are inherently different from APIs in a local library.

If we continue to use synchronous approach, then network delays (seconds or even minutes) add to the time it takes to execute the API, before the control returns. What happens to our application thread in the meantime – well it blocks. Such blocking calls are undesirable in most situations including our WinForm application. If you run the application and try to do "many to many" rate conversion, you will notice that the User Interface stops responding to our mouse clicks. This is because we have called synchronous version of the API — **GetCurrencyBySymbol( )**. Note that call to this API is made inside our WinForm's event loop (Go button's click event handler). As a result, no other WinForm events will be processed until conversion rates for all currencies have been found. This establishes the need for making use of the asynchronous version — **GetCurrencyBySymbolAsync( )** instead.

This may lead you to believe that you must always make use of asynchronous version of the web service API. That however is not always the case. In fact which version to use, varies from one situation to another. Let's consider an example. Consider the APIs **GetCountryNames( )**. We have called this API during the loading of WinForm. Needless to say, we have used synchronous version of this API. Wouldn't this be an issue? If you think about it carefully, you would make following observations:

(a) We call this API only twice – that too during loading of a form. Thereafter, we use the same result as source and destination country names as long as application is running.
(b) Implementation of this API on the server side is likely to be faster as the data it returns is nearly static – country names don't change every day.

Besides, even if we had used asynchronous version of this API we wouldn't have gained much. This is because, unless the country names are available, there isn't anything useful that you can do with the WinForm. So, this is the perfect case for using the synchronous approach.

Hence, in general in situations where result(s) of an API call are not immediately required, asynchronous approach would make more sense. This approach usually leads to better performance and better responsiveness of the application. On the flip side, asynchronous approach is more complex to understand and is trickier to implement.

Moral is, the way "One size fits all" formula doesn't work in real life, so is the case with web services programming models. So our prayer should be, "God, give me the prudence to use the right approach in a given situation ". We hope to build this prudence in the next chapter of this series.

Chapter 4: Asynchronous Web Services Client   25

4

Asynchronous Web Services client

ASP.Net Web Services

God has blessed human beings with the ability to perform several tasks concurrently. That is why we are able to drive a car, listen to music, follow the traffic rules, talk to the co-passengers—all this without losing the mains focus, i.e. driving. Since programmers are human beings and programming is the art of solving people's problems, it is only natural that programmers have evolved mechanisms to perform several activities concurrently. Opportunity for use parallelism exists quite naturally in web service applications. In this chapter we will try and capture this theme.

Understanding Approaches

Web Service API stubs in proxy class are generated auto-magically by **wsdl.exe**. It generates both synchronous and asynchronous flavors of each web service API. The web service implementation has no knowledge of asynchronous APIs. For example, **GetRateBySymbol( )** has following forms in proxy class:

```
(a)   public float GetRateBySymbol ( string from, string to )
(b)   public float GetRateBySymbolAsync ( string from,
                  string to, object state )
(c)   public float GetRateBySymbolAsync ( string from,
                                          string to )
```

First API is the synchronous version. It sends a request to the server, waits for the response and then returns the result. Figure 1 shows how this happens.

Chapter 4: Asynchronous Web Services Client

Synchronous Call

doConversion( )
```
for ( .. ; .. ; .. )
{
  GetRateBySymbol( ) ;
}
```

Proxy Class
```
GetRateBySymbol ( .., .. )
{
  ...
}
```

CurrencyService
```
GetRateBySymbol ( .., .. )
{
  ...
}
```

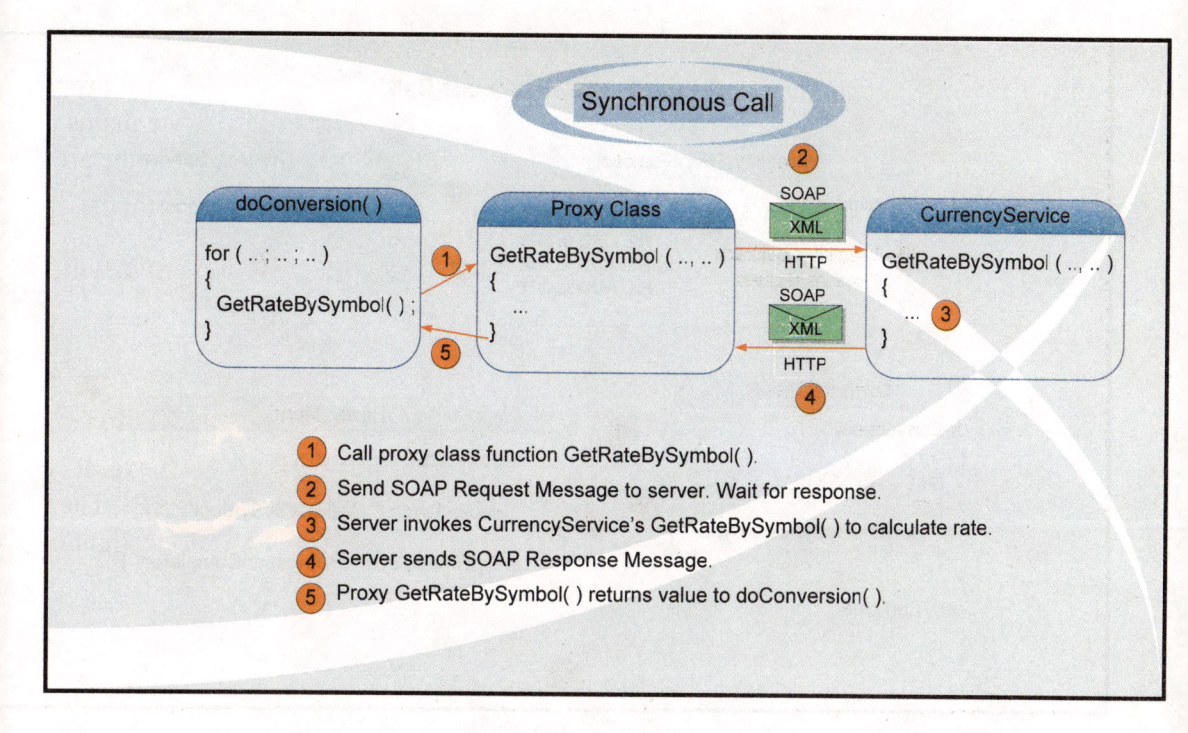

1. Call proxy class function GetRateBySymbol( ).
2. Send SOAP Request Message to server. Wait for response.
3. Server invokes CurrencyService's GetRateBySymbol( ) to calculate rate.
4. Server sends SOAP Response Message.
5. Proxy GetRateBySymbol( ) returns value to doConversion( ).

Figure 4.1 – Synchronous call to web service API

As shown in Figure 4.1, call to API **GetRateBySymbol( )** is routed to the proxy class on client machine. Proxy class converts this API call into XML based SOAP message envelope and passes it to the server over HTTP transport. SOAP message envelope is unmarshalled on the server and then CurrencyService's **GetRateBySymbol( )** is called. This function obtains latest currency conversion rate. Only after the rate is obtained, control returns to the client. On the client (which was waiting for the response), return values are unmarshalled from SOAP message envelope. Finally, control returns to **doConversion( )**.

Asynchronous Approach

APIs (b) and (c) mentioned are implemented in the proxy class to facilitate asynchronous calls. When we call these APIs, control returns immediately, without waiting for the result of the operation. Once the control returns, the user is free to interact with the WinForm. A lot of things happen under the hood to facilitate this. These steps are outlined in Figure 4.2. Take a close look at it, as the explanation that follows refers to it.

28   ASP.Net Web Services

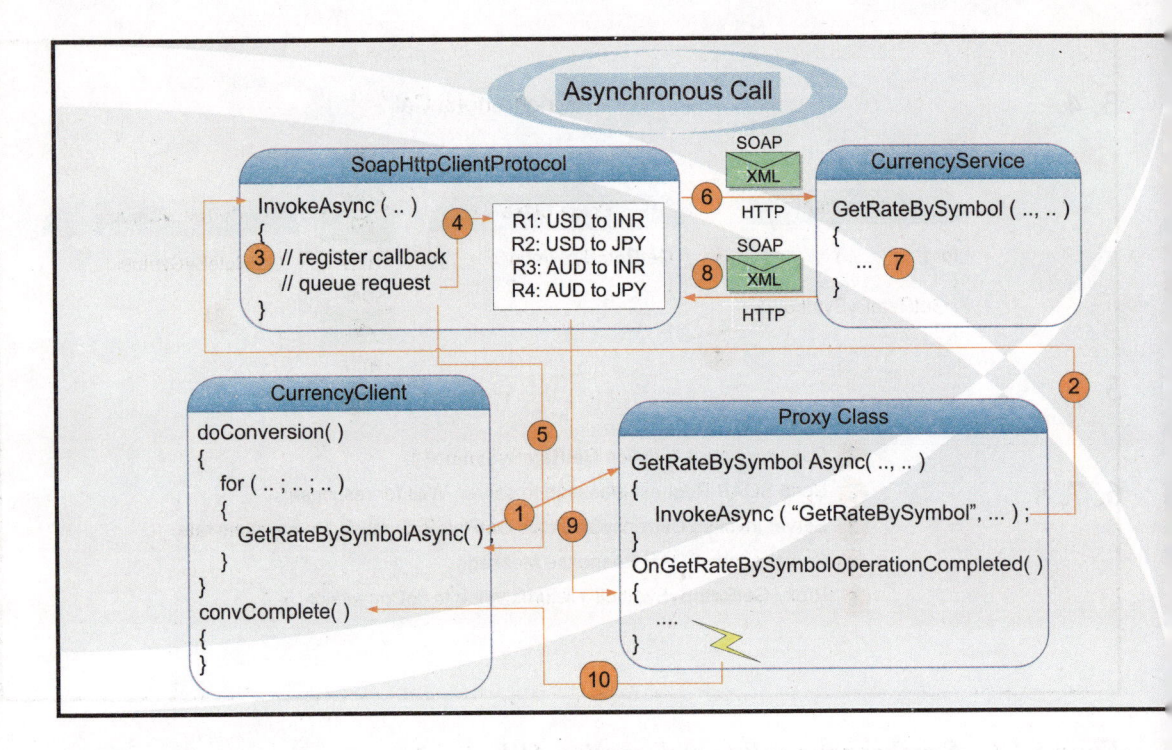

Figure 4.2 – Asynchronous call to web service API

Given below is the sequence of steps that are carried out when the client uses the asynchronous APIs :

Step Number	Details
1	**doConversion( )** function calls the API **GetRateBySymbolAsync( )**.
2	**GetRateBySymbolAsync( )** calls base class function **InvokeAsync( )**. Note that the proxy class is derived from **SoapHttpClientProtocol** class present in FCL. While making the call, three parameters are passed to it: - Name of the web service API – **GetRateBySymbol**. - Array of the arguments for this API – (**fromC, toC**). - Address of callback function **OnGetRateBySymbolOperationCompleted( )**. Role of this

Chapter 4: Asynchronous Web Services Client

	function is explained in step ⑨.
3, 4	**InvokeAsync( )** API the heart of asynchronous approach. It performs two jobs: - It registers the address of callback function passed to it for this request. - It queues the request for execution of the web service API **GetRateBySymbol**.
5	The control returns from **InvokeAsync( )** back to **GetRateBySymbolAsync( )**. and finally to **doConversion( )**.
6, 7, 8	In addition to the **GetRateBySymbol**, there might be requests for other web service APIs in the same quest. Requests in the queue are executed in the context of separate worker threads. Note that these worker threads themselves use synchronous approach to communication with the server. Although we can make intelligent guesses about how this works, implementation details are hidden inside **InvokeAsync( )**. Server is completely unaware of the fact that these requests are being made by an asynchronous client.
9	As each request is completed, the callback function registered for that request is invoked. Result of the API call is passed as an argument to the callback function.
10	In our case, the callback function is **OnGetRateBySymbolOperationCompleted( )**. It generates an event to notify the client about completion of asynchronous API call and availability of results. The result of the operation are passed to the event handler using object of class **GetRateBySymbolCompletedEventArgs**. This class is also generated by **wsdl.exe**. Our event handler **convComplete( )** displays the result of operation in **ResultBox** textbox.

Note that, **InvokeAsync( )** is a common function for asynchronous invocation for every web service API. It registers the callback and queues the API request for each API in the web service.

Implementing Asynchronous Client

Rather than showing you all the code for an asynchronous client, we will show you the changes that we need to make to the WinForm client that we have developed earlier. The first change we need to make is in the constructor. This change is shown below.

```csharp
public CurrencyClient( )
{
    // Existing code
    service.GetRateBySymbolCompleted +=
    new GetRateBySymbolCompletedEventHandler ( convComplete ) ;
}
```

As shown here, we have added an event handler for asynchronous version of **GetRateBySymbol** API. Implementation of **convComplete( )** is discussed later.

Now we need to change **doConversion( )** to use asynchronous approach. The code for it is shown below:

```csharp
private void doConversion( )
{
  if ( FromList.SelectedItems.Count == 0 ||
       ToList.SelectedItems.Count == 0 )
    return;

  ResultBox.Text = "" ;
  showProgressBar( ) ;

  for ( int i = 0 ; i < FromList.SelectedItems.Count ; i++ )
  {
     string from = FromList.SelectedItems[ i ].ToString( ) ;
     CountryCurrency fromC = countries[ from ] ;

     for ( int j = 0 ; j < ToList.SelectedItems.Count ; j++ )
     {
```

Chapter 4: Asynchronous Web Services Client 31

```
        string to = ToList.SelectedItems[ j ].ToString( ) ;
        CountryCurrency toC = countries[ to ] ;
        convertOne ( fromC, toC ) ;
      }

   }
}
```

Here, to begin with, we have called **showProgressBar( )** function to set the limits for progress bar displayed during the operation as shown below:

```
private void showProgressBar( )
{
   ConversionProgress.Minimum = 1 ;
   ConversionProgress.Maximum = FromList.SelectedItems.Count *
                                 ToList.SelectedItems.Count ;
   ConversionProgress.Value = ConversionProgress.Minimum ;
   ConversionProgress.Visible = true ;
}
```

Next, we have called the **convertOne( )** function for each desired pair of conversion. It calls **GetRateBySymbolAsync( )** to do the actual conversion. The result of conversion is known only when "conversion complete" event is received. Third argument passed to **GetRateBySymbolAsync( )** helps us to correlate the result of operation with unique source and target currencies. This argument is returned to us in "conversion complete" event handler discussed later.

```
private void convertOne ( CountryCurrency fromC,
                          CountryCurrency toC )
{
   pending++ ;
   service.GetRateBySymbolAsync ( fromC.symbol, toC.symbol,
                   new ConversionPair ( fromC, toC ) ) ;
}

class ConversionPair
```

```
{
   public CountryCurrency fromC ;
   public CountryCurrency toC ;

   public ConversionPair ( CountryCurrency f, CountryCurrency t
)
   {
      fromC = f ;
      toC = t ;
   }
}
```

When all asynchronous requests have been generated, **doConversion( )** returns. For each asynchronous API call, result of conversion is made available through the event handler **convComplete( )** shown below:

```
private void convComplete ( object sender,
GetRateBySymbolCompletedEventArgs e )
{
   ConversionPair p = ( ConversionPair ) e.UserState ;

   if ( e.Error == null )
   {
      ResultBox.Text +=
         String.Format ( "1 {0}{1} = {2} {3}{4}" +
                  Environment.NewLine, p.fromC.country,
                  p.fromC.currency, e.Result, p.toC.country,
                  p.toC.currency ) ;
      ResultBox.ScrollToCaret( ) ;
   }
   else
   {
      ResultBox.Text += "Failed: " + p.fromC.country + ", " +
                        p.toC.country + Environment.NewLine
                  ;
   }
}
```

Chapter 4: Asynchronous Web Services Client 33

```
    ConversionProgress.PerformStep( ) ;
    pending-- ;

    if ( pending == 0 )
    {
      ConversionProgress.Visible = false ;
      GoButton.Enabled = true ;
    }
  }
}
```

All that we have done here is, obtain the state object we had passed in call to **GetRateBySymbolAsync( )**. This tells us which currency pair's conversion rate is now available. Rate of conversion is extracted from the field **Result** and then displayed in the **ResultBox**. Note that only if the **Error** field is **null**, operation is considered successful. Otherwise a reference to exception object would be stored in this field. This can be used to find the details about the error. The progress bar is suitably updated.

Now build and run the application. If you select America and Australia from the source listbox and India and Japan from the target listbox, and click Go button, then the conversion rates would be displayed in the **ResultBox** as shown in Figure 4.3. During the conversion, we can display a progress bar to give visual feedback to the user.

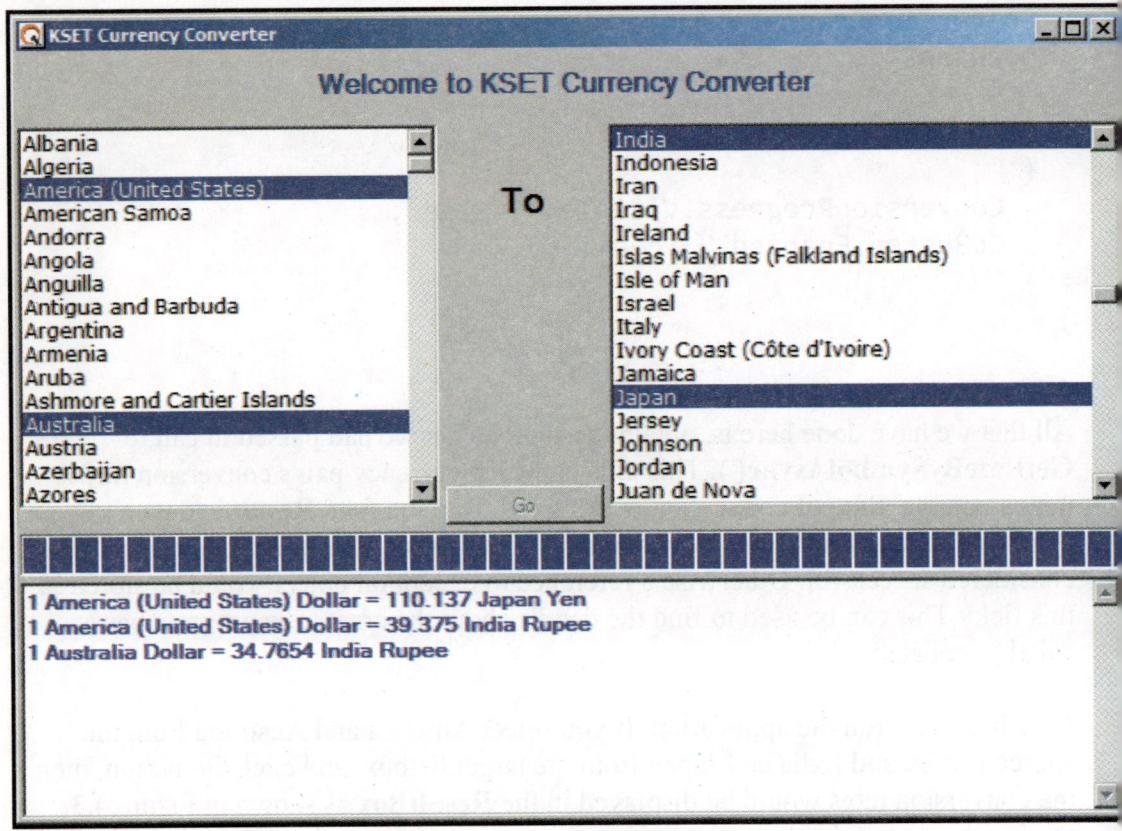

Figure 4.3 – Conversion rates for many to many

5

Creating Currency Web Service

Using a published web service is one part of the story. Other part that makes the story complete is the creating of a web service. We have spent enough time wetting our feet in understanding how to use a web service. It's about time that we take a deep dive and see how to create a web service.

Why Create A Web Service?

There is no dearth of articles, tutorials and books that explain how to create a web service. When we started exploring web services, we took a good look at them. There are very many examples explaining creation of web services to convert temperature from Centigrade to Fahrenheit, add / subtract / multiply or divide two numbers, Metric to US unit conversion etc. Most of them seem to have adopted a cookbook approach to creation of web services. We couldn't get convinced that for performing operations mentioned above, we have to even write a web service in the first place. That set us thinking as to what is rationale behind writing web services. After some thinking, we realized that motivation for writing a web service could be one or more of the following:

Automation:

Because of Internet, most web applications today are purely interactive. For example, to search a term and find the results requires use of mouse and keyboard inside a browser. If we need same functionality programmatically, there is rarely a way to do so. Companies like Google and Amazon have created web search and book search related web services to do precisely this kind of automation.

Live data:

Many businesses need data that changes periodically. For example, stock price of publicly traded companies like Sony, Cannon, Hitachi, or weather information of various cities or Electrical energy generation data at various stations in a country, etc. If your application needs such kind of data, ideally, there should be a programmatic way of retrieving it.

B2B integration:

In a B2B scenario it is possible that the applications written in different languages, running on different platforms wish to communicate with one another. For example, a .NET WinForm / WebForm application running on Wintel platform may wish to

Chapter 5: Creating Currency Web Service

communicate with the code written in Java running on a Linux machine. In such a case, if the Java code is written and exposed as a web service then this B2B integration would be easier.

Revenue generation:

Web services offer an opportunity to expose useful functionality for consumption by disparate users and evolve different revenue models around it. For example, a web service publisher may charge its users on a lump sum basis or on a per usage basis.

Hence we decided to write a web service that would meet at least some of the above requirements. For data driven web sites that involve monetary transactions on an international scale it would be necessary to get the latest currency conversion rates at the point in time when the transaction takes place. The Currency Service that we intend to create now would serve this purpose very well.

The Currency Web Service

Before we get into the nitty-gritty's of the Currency web service code please bear the following things in mind:

(a)   The up-to-date currency conversion rates are available at www.xe.com.
(b)   Currency service should communicate with this site to obtain the conversion rates.

To begin with, create the Currency web service by following two simple steps mentioned below:

(a)   Select File | New Web Site | ASP.NET Web Service from the menu.
(b)   Give the location and name of the web service (Currency).

On doing so, the following skeleton code gets created:

```
using System ;
using System.Web ;
using System.Web.Services ;
using System.Web.Services.Protocols ;
```

```csharp
[WebService(Namespace = "http://tempuri.org/")]
[WebServiceBinding(ConformsTo = WsiProfiles.BasicProfile1_1)]
public class CurrencyService : System.Web.Services.WebService
{
    public CurrencyService( )
    {
    }

    [WebMethod]
    public string HelloWorld( )
    {
        return "Hello World" ;
    }
}
```

As you can see, the code contains a class called **CurrencyService** derived from **WebService** class and it contains a constructor and a method called **HelloWorld( )**. The **CurrencyService** class has two attributes.

```csharp
[WebService(Namespace = "http://tempuri.org/")]
[WebServiceBinding(ConformsTo = WsiProfiles.BasicProfile1_1)]
```

Of these, the **WebService** attribute allows you to specifiy the namespace to which the CurrencyService belongs. It is a good idea to use your company's domain name in the namespace to ensure uniqueness of your service. Hence we have replaced the original namespace identifier with http://quest.ksetindia.com/services/CurrencyService. So the new attribute now looks like:

```csharp
[WebService(Namespace =
"http://quest.ksetindia.com/services/CurrencyService/")]
```

The second attribute indicates conformance to an emerging web services standard that ensures better interoperability amongst services developed and deployed on different platforms.

Chapter 5: Creating Currency Web Service 39

The method **HelloWorld( )** has a attribute called **[WebMethod]** which marks it as a web service API method. We should delete this method and add the following web methods to the code:

```
- CountryCurrency GetCurrency ( String cname )
- float GetRateByCountry ( String from, String to )
- float GetRateBySymbol ( String from, String to )
- String [ ] GetCountryNames( )
- CountryCurrency [ ] GetCountryCurrencies( )
```

Do ensure that you mark each of these methods with the **[WebMethod]** attribute. As you can notice a type **CountryCurrency** is being returned by some of these methods. So we should define it as a public type so that it becomes available to the clients of this web service. The code for **CountryCurrency** type is shown below:

```
public class CountryCurrency
{
  public String country ;
  public String currency ;
  public String symbol ;


  // 0-arg. constructor is necessary for serialization
  public CountryCurrency( )
  {
  }

  public CountryCurrency( String n, String cname, String csym)
  {
     country = n ;
     this.currency = cname ;
     this.symbol = csym ;
  }
}
```

CurrencyService Methods

Let us now implement the web methods that already stand added. Before we do that, we need to add a private method called **MapCountry( )** to the **CurrencyService** class. Its code is given below:

```
private Dictionary<String, CountryCurrency> MapCountry( )
{
    WebRequest req = WebRequest.Create (
                        "http://www.xe.com/ucc/full.php" )
                     ;
    WebResponse resp = req.GetResponse ( ) ;
    StreamReader sr ;
    sr = new StreamReader ( resp.GetResponseStream( ) ) ;
    String respStr = sr.ReadToEnd( ) ;
    StringBuilder sb = new StringBuilder( ) ;
    String reExp = "<option
            value=\"(.+)\">(.*),(.+)\\s\\(.*\\)</option>" ;
    Match m = Regex.Match ( respStr, reExp ) ;

    Dictionary<String, CountryCurrency> ctsym =
        new Dictionary<String, CountryCurrency>( ) ;

    while ( m.Success )
    {
      if ( !ctsym.ContainsKey ( m.Groups[ 2 ].Value ) )
        ctsym.Add ( m.Groups[ 2 ].Value,
          new CountryCurrency ( m.Groups[ 2 ].Value,
            m.Groups [ 3 ].Value, m.Groups [ 1 ].Value ) ) ;
      m = m.NextMatch( ) ;
    }

    return ctsym ;
}
```

As discussed earlier, our only access to up-to-date information on currency rates and the countries list is a portal—www.xe.com. As a first step, we have extracted the list

Chapter 5: Creating Currency Web Service   41

of country names, currency symbol and currency name from a standard web page http://www.xe.com/ucc/full.php on this portal. As you will agree, we must load the page and parse out the desired information in a completely automated manner. Towards this end, we have used **WebRequest** and **WebResonse** classes to retrieve the HTML text for this web page. Once retrieved, we have parsed the HTML using Standard Regular Expressions which offer a very powerful mechanism for text processing. For fast lookup of currency information for a country we have created a dictionary with country name as the key and its **CountryCurrency** object as value.

Let us now turn our attention to the most important web method, namely **GetRateBySymbol( )**. This is the method that actually gets the live conversion rates. Here too we have built a web request and retrieved the HTML data. However, what makes this method different is that the URL that we use is constructed dynamically to encode from and to currency symbols for the desired conversion. Whenever we use this automation approach, first task is to know how to pass parameters to a web request. In some cases, HTTP GET request can be used, while in other HTTP POST request has to be used. In this case, we have used a GET request. The regular expression used to parse the response has been carefully chosen to extract the conversion rate. This method is shown below:

```
[WebMethod]
public float GetRateBySymbol ( String from, String to )
{
  String URL = String.Format (
 "http://www.xe.com/ucc/convert.cgi?Amount=1&From={0}&To={1}",
            from, to ) ;

  WebRequest req = WebRequest.Create ( URL ) ;
  WebResponse resp = req.GetResponse( ) ;
  StreamReader sr ;

  sr = new StreamReader ( resp.GetResponseStream( ) ) ;
  String respStr = sr.ReadToEnd( ) ;
  String reExp =
    String.Format ( @"[0-9.]+\s*{0}\s*=\s*([0-9.,]+)\s{1}",
                    from, to ) ;
  Match m = Regex.Match ( respStr, reExp ) ;
  String x = m.Groups [ 1 ].Value ;
```

```
    return float.Parse ( x ) ;
}
```

The next two methods are quite simple. The **GetCurrency( )** method returns the **CountryCurrrency** object for the specified country name. **GetRateByCountry( )** is similar to **GetRateBySymbol( )**, except that it returns the conversion based on country rates rather than currency symbols. Both these web methods are shown below:

```
[WebMethod]
public CountryCurrency GetCurrency ( String cname )
{
    Dictionary<String, CountryCurrency> cmap = MapCountry( ) ;

    if ( cmap.ContainsKey ( cname ) )
        return cmap [ cname ] ;

    return null ;
}

[WebMethod]
public float GetRateByCountry ( String from, String to )
{
    return GetRateBySymbol ( GetCurrency ( from ).symbol,
                            GetCurrency ( to ).symbol ) ;
}
```

As the name suggests, **GetCountryNames( )** method returns an array of strings containing names of all recognized nations of the world. It uses **MapCountry( )** helper function to get this information. Clients need this API to know the exact strings for names of the countries for use with other APIs in the web service. For example, it helps get the right name out of USA, U.S.A, US of America, United States, etc.

Chapter 5: Creating Currency Web Service

```
[WebMethod]
public String[ ] GetCountryNames( )
{
   String[ ] keys = new String [ MapCountry ( ).Keys.Count ] ;
   Dictionary<String, CountryCurrency>.KeyCollection.Enumerator
      ke = MapCountry( ).Keys.GetEnumerator( ) ;

   int i = 0 ;

   while ( ke.MoveNext( ) )
     keys[ i++ ] = ke.Current ;

   return keys ;
}
```

Lastly, the method **GetCountryCurrencies( )** returns detailed information of each country's currency as shown below.

```
[WebMethod]
public CountryCurrency[ ] GetCountryCurrencies( )
{
   CountryCurrency [ ] map =
      new CountryCurrency [ MapCountry ( ).Keys.Count ] ;

   Dictionary<String, CountryCurrency>.Enumerator ke =
      MapCountry( ).GetEnumerator( ) ;

   int i = 0 ;

   while ( ke.MoveNext( ) )
     map[ i++ ] = ke.Current.Value ;

   return map ;
}
```

Chapter 6: Nuances of Web Services 45

6
Nuances of Web Services

Training your troops for a battle is not enough to ensure success in the battlefield. Unless the troops are put through fire in War Games and simulated battlefields, success is hardly guaranteed. Any good army General knows this. Same is true about web services. Once they are out on the Internet, your prestige on the line. Hence, every experienced web developer has to create a near real life environment to test his web service before publishing it on Internet. In this article, we will show you how to create an environment for building mission critical web services. You will also agree that in life, getting correct results alone is not enough. How efficiently you get those results, separates men from boys. Web services are no different. This article also explores how to implement web services efficiently.

Debugging A Web Service

When we created the **CurrencyService** we had given the location name as http://localhost/CurrencyService. As a result, our web service gets hosted in the local IIS (Internet Information Server) in a directory C:\Inetpub\wwwroot\CurrencyService. Once we have compiled the web service successfully from this location we need to test and debug it. This requires two important steps:

(a)   Enable Integrated Authentication in local IIS Server
(b)   Change Web Reference in Client Application

Following sections describe these steps in detail.

IIS Server Configuration

IIS Server configuration steps are as follows:

(a)   Open Start | Settings | Control Panel | Administrative Tools | Internet Information Services.
(b)   Expand the Web Sites node select "Default Web Site" node.
(c)   Select Action | Properties menu item. A dialog will appear.
(d)   Click on "Directory Security" tab, followed by Edit button.

Chapter 6: Nuances of Web Services 47

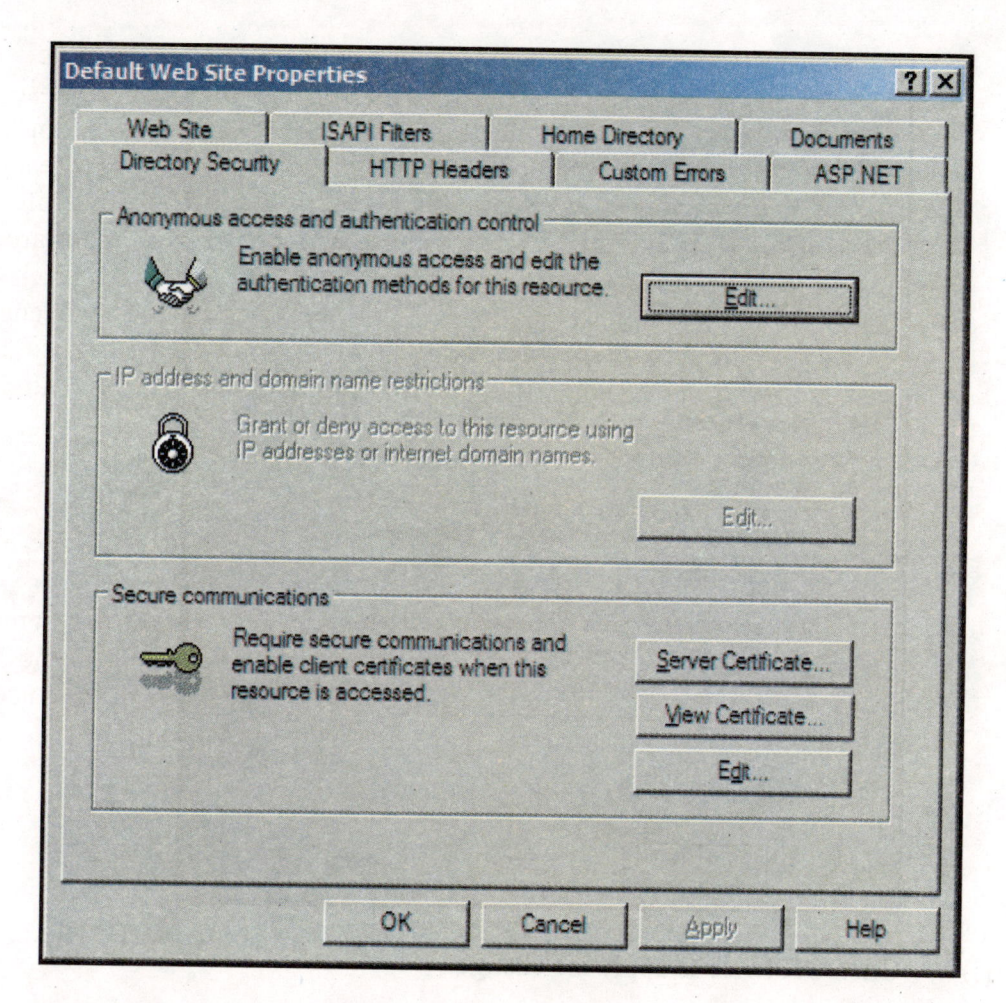

(e) Under "Authentication Methods", select "Integrated Windows Authentication" radio button if it's not already selected.

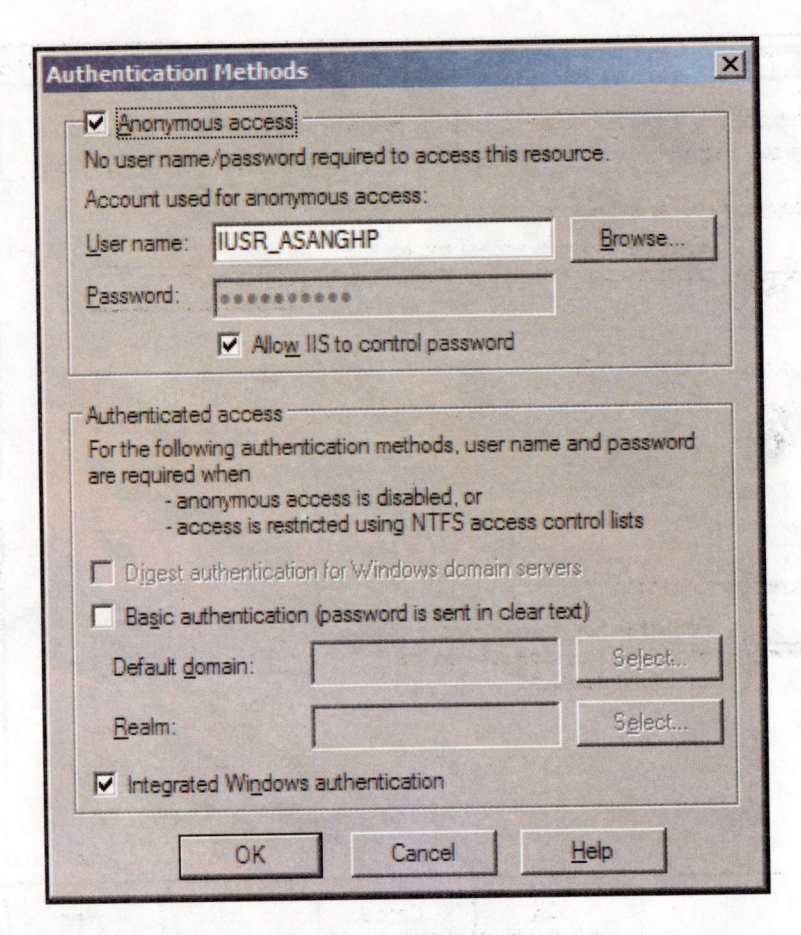

(f)   Click OK twice to apply the changes.

Now start the web service using 'Debug | Start Debugging' menu option in Visual Studio and set breakpoints in some of methods of CurrencyService. Once this is done, you can run the client application to test this web service.

Change Web Reference In Client Application

The steps to change the Web Reference are as follows:

(a)   Expand CurrencyClient02 node in solution explorer window.
(b)   Expand Web References node and select com.ksetindia.ws.currency.
(c)   In the properties window, change 'Web Reference URL' field to:
      http://localhost/CurrencyService/CurrencyService.asmx?WSDL
(d)   Choose Project | Update Web Reference.

Chapter 6: Nuances of Web Services 49

Do realize that the settings mentioned above are critical in ensuring that our web service implementation is robust. We have noticed that people often skip these steps and straightaway publish the service with minimal testing. In our opinion this is a "penny wise, pound foolish" approach. Note that unless we make these settings, we would not be able to create a near real environment in which we test and debug the service. Any experienced web developer would give his right arm to setup an environment which lets the developer debug the implementation in all possible ways before final deployment on production server.

We are now finally ready to test and debug our web service. Launch the client application. You will notice that the control halts at the breakpoints you have set, when client sends rate conversion requests to it.

Performance Tuning

Once we are sure that the web service has been thoroughly tested for correctness, we should concentrate on is its performance. A closer look at CurrencyService can easily lead you to the following conclusions:

(a) APIs like **GetCountryNames( )** and **GetCountryCurrencies( )** return same result every time they are called.
(b) APIs like **GetRateBySymbol( )** and **GetRateByCountry( )** return a rate that changes once every minute for a given pair of currencies/symbols.

Luckily for us, ASP.NET 2.0 framework allows us to hold requests and responses for APIs of our choice in server's memory. This process is known as caching. Note that these requests are not cached eternally. They remain in memory only for the duration that we specify. Best of all, enabling caching doesn't require any code change other than passing a parameter **CacheDuration** to the **WebMethod** attribute. This is shown below:

```
[WebMethod ( CacheDuration = 10000 )]
public String[ ] GetCountryCurrencies( )
{
   CountryCurrency[ ] map =
       new CountryCurrency[ MapCountry( ).Keys.Count ] ;

   Dictionary<String, CountryCurrency>.Enumerator ke =
```

```
    MapCountry ( ).GetEnumerator( ) ;

  int i = 0 ;
  while ( ke.MoveNext( ) )
    map [ i++ ] = ke.Current.Value ;

  return map ;
}

[WebMethod ( CacheDuration = 60 )]
public float GetRateBySymbol ( String from, String to )
{
  if ( Session == null || (string)Session [ "apikey" ] !=
                                                 secretKey )
    return -1.0f ;

  String URL = String.Format (
  "http://www.xe.com/ucc/convert.cgi?Amount=1&From={0}&To={1}",
       from, to ) ;

  WebRequest req = WebRequest.Create ( URL ) ;
  WebResponse resp = req.GetResponse( ) ;
  StreamReader sr ;

  sr = new StreamReader ( resp.GetResponseStream( ) ) ;
  String respStr = sr.ReadToEnd( ) ;

  // Live rates at 2007.12.19 05:10:33 UTC
  String reExp =
  String.Format ( @"[0-9.]+\s*{0}\s*=\s*([0-9.,]+)\s{1}",
                    from, to ) ;

  Match m = Regex.Match ( respStr, reExp ) ;
  String x = m.Groups [ 1 ].Value ;
  return float.Parse ( x ) ;
}
```

Note that we have used very different **CacheDuration** values for these methods. This has been done keeping in mind the nature of these APIs. Once you make these changes and test the **CurrencyService** again, you can notice a significant change in client's performance.

It is important to realize that overzealous use of caching can put tremendous pressure on server's memory. Hence prudence must be exercised while deciding what to cache and how long to cache it for. Secondly, caching should not compromise the liveness of responses returned by our APIs. For example, if currency rates are fluctuating at intervals shorter than a minute the duration of caching must be reduced to ensure more up-to-date results.

Chapter 7: Show Me The Money!

7
Show Me The Money!

Every inventor dreams of creating something will change people's lives. When finally he/she gets there, one important issue remains – does he benefit from the discovery or not? Web Service developers strive to do something similar. After creating something good, you should be able to benefit from it financially. Thus it is important to be able to build a revenue model around your web service. This article will show you how.

Let us see how simple it is to create a revenue model around our **CurrencyService**. Out of the five methods that are provided by this service, we can charge users for using the most important APIs—**GetRateBySymbol( )** and **GetRateByCountry( )**. To convince users to pay for the service, it would be a nice idea to return some more useful information to our subscribers. This information can be the exact time at which conversion rate was obtained from the marketplace. This will be of great importance to currency traders whose business depends on the "liveness" of data. To achieve this, we will use ability of ASP.NET web services to exchange SOAP headers between client and server. Figure 7.1 shows the workflow that we propose to use for our revenue based implementation.

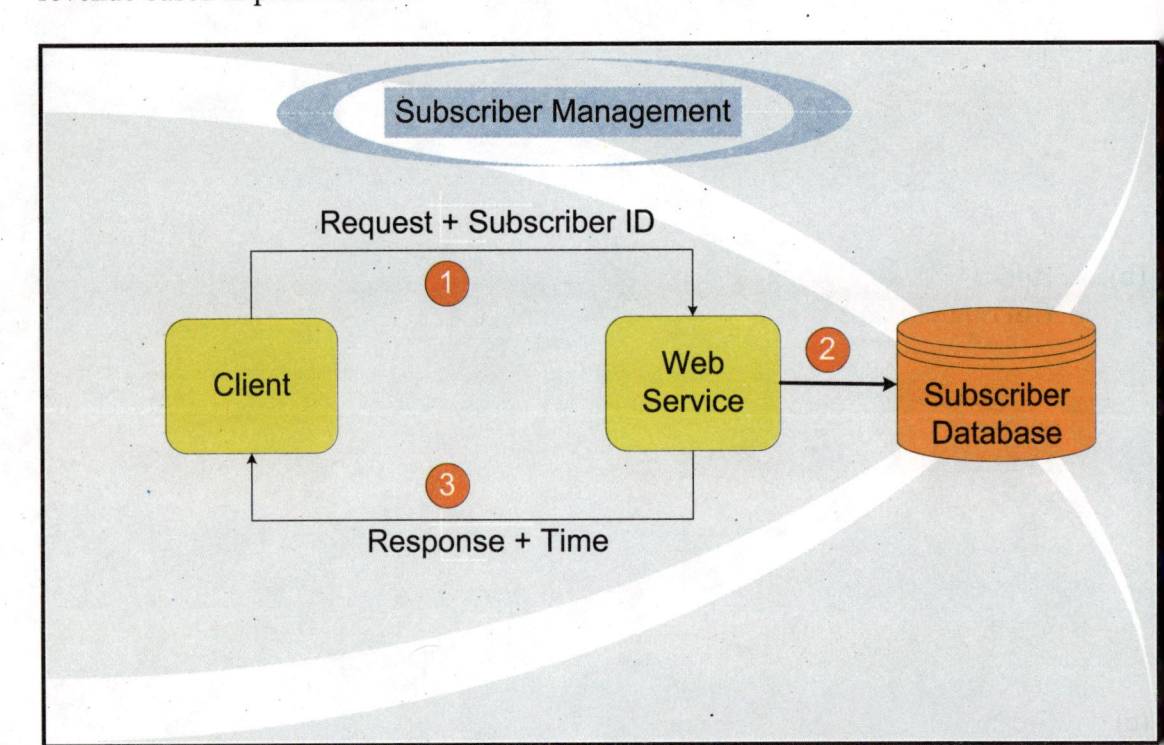

Figure 7.1: Web Service Revenue Model Workflow

Chapter 7: Show Me The Money! 55

Each subscriber will be assigned a unique 128-bit identifier. These identifiers would be stored in a specially created subscriber database. Each time the subscriber calls either **GetRateBySymbol( )** or **GetRateByCountry( )** his unique id would be passed to them. Note that the id would be passed through a SOAP header and not as a method parameter. In the method it would be verified from the database whether the id is valid and the subscription has not expired. If any of these conditions fail then an error is returned. Otherwise, the method would be executed and the conversion rate would be returned. In the response the time at which the conversion rate was obtained would also be returned via the SOAP header.

Let us now see the steps involved in implementing this model in **CurrencyService**. These are described below.

(a) Create a public class **SubscriberHeader** that inherits from **SoapHeader**.

```
public class SubscriberHeader : SoapHeader
{
   public string id ;
   public DateTime serverTime ;
}
```

(b) Add a public variable **subscriberKey** of type **KeyHeader** in **CurrencyService** class.

```
public class CurrencyService :
System.Web.Services.WebService
{
   public SubscriberHeader sHeader ;
   // ...
}
```

(c) Create Subscriber database using MS SQL Server 2005 Express Edition. Figure 7.2 shows the schema for this database.

```
┌─────────────────┐              ┌─────────────────┐
│   Subscriber    │              │ SubscriberStatus│
├─────┬───────────┤              ├─────┬───────────┤
│ PK  │ SubId     │─────────────▶│ PK  │ StatusId  │
├─────┼───────────┤              ├─────┼───────────┤
│     │ Name      │              │     │ Name      │
│ FK1 │ Status    │              │     │           │
└─────┴───────────┘              └─────┴───────────┘
```

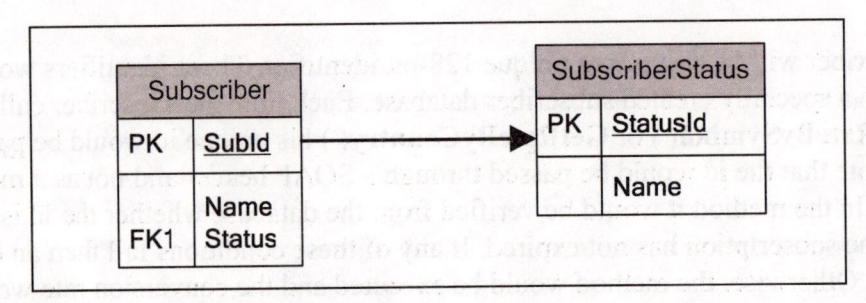

Figure 7.2: Subscriber Database

As you will notice, SubId is the unique identifier assigned to each developer. This 128-bit ID is generated using SQL server function **NEWID( )** while inserting a new subscriber in the database. The **Status** table maintains mapping from numeric status value to its string representation – e.g. 1 – Disabled, 2 – Enabled etc. We can easily create a simple ASP.NET Web Application to manage this Subscriber database. However, that's hardly the point here. So we recommend that you directly use Visual Studio 2005 Data Designer to insert some initial entries in this database. We have created two subscribers – Jayant and Hirohito. One of them is disabled while other is enabled. Figures 7.3 & 7.4 show the details.

SubId	Name	Status
95e62420-d529-49f4-ba79-151df61ac788	Hirohito	2
ce55bd21-2948-40e0-aa26-86b37298d064	Jayant	1
NULL	NULL	NULL

Figure 7.3: Subscriber Table Data

StatusId	Name
1	Disabled
2	Enabled
NULL	NULL

Figure 7.4: SubscriberStatus Table Data

(d) To programmatically access the database through our web service we need to create a database adapter. This is done by adding a dataset to our web service.

Chapter 7: Show Me The Money! 57

For this right click on **App_code** node in Solution Explorer and choose 'Add New Item'. In the dialog that appears, select Dataset as the item type and choose SubscriberDS.xsd as the name of this dataset.

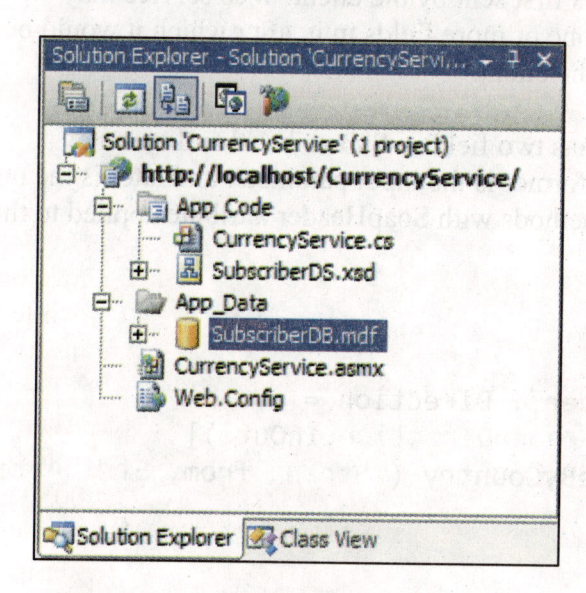

Figure 7.5: Subscriber DataSet

(e) Now we need to add a simply query **GetStatusById** to this dataset. Figure 7.6 shows this query. This query will allow us to validate subscriber id and his status.

```
SELECT SubscriberStatus.Name
FROM Subscriber, SubscriberStatus
WHERE (SubId = @SubId) AND
( Subscriber.Status =
    SubscriberStatus.StatusId)
```

Figure 7.6: Query for Subscriber validation

(f) Now we need to attach a **SoapHeader** attribute to methods **GetRateBySymbol( )** and **GetRateByCountry( )** and validate the call to these methods. **SoapHeader** attribute specifies the name of the variable (**sHeader**) in which the received header will be copied. We can specify the direction for SOAP header. Direction can be one of the following:

- Input: Client sends the header to the web service
- Output: Web service constructs the header and returns it to the client
- InputOutput: The header is first sent by the client. Web service may manipulate one or more fields in it, after which it would be returned to the client.

In our case, SOAP header has two fields—SubscriberId and currency conversion time. Of these, former is the input parameter and later is the output parameter. The modified methods with SoapHeader attribute applied to them are shown below:

```
[WebMethod]
[SoapHeader ( "sHeader", Direction =
            SoapHeaderDirection.InOut )]
public float GetRateByCountry ( String from, String to )
{
  try
  {
    return GetRateBySymbol (
        GetCurrency ( from ).symbol,
        GetCurrency ( to ).symbol ) ;
  }
  catch ( Exception ex )
  {
    return -1.0f ;
  }
}

[WebMethod (CacheDuration = 60) ]
[SoapHeader ( "sHeader", Direction =
            SoapHeaderDirection.InOut )]
public float GetRateBySymbol ( String from, String to )
{
  if ( ! ValidateSubscriber ( sHeader ) )
    return -1.0f ;

  String URL = String.Format (
```

Chapter 7: Show Me The Money!   59

```csharp
"http://www.xe.com/ucc/convert.cgi?Amount=1&From={0}&To={1}",
    from, to ) ;
WebRequest req = WebRequest.Create ( URL ) ;
WebResponse resp = req.GetResponse( ) ;
StreamReader sr ;
sr = new StreamReader ( resp.GetResponseStream( ) ) ;
String respStr = sr.ReadToEnd( ) ;

// Live rates at 2007.12.19 05:10:33 UTC
Match m = Regex.Match ( respStr,
                    @"Live\srates\sat\s(.+)UTC" ) ;
sHeader.serverTime = DateTime.Parse ( m.Groups [ 1 ].
                    Value ).ToLocalTime( ) ;
String reExp =
String.Format ( @"[0-9.]+\s*{0}\s*=\s*([0-9.,]+)\s{1}",
    from, to ) ;
m = Regex.Match ( respStr, reExp ) ;
String x = m.Groups [ 1 ].Value ;
return float.Parse ( x ) ;
}
```

The **GetRateByCountry( )** method is same as before except for the addition of SoapHeader attribute. In **GetRateBySymbol( )** we have added the code for:

- Validating the user by calling **ValidateSubscriber( )**.
- Obtaining the currency conversion time and assigning it to the SOAP header field **serverTime**.

(g) The **ValidateSubscriber( )** function uses the database adapter class created earlier using the **SubscriberDS** dataset and calls **GetStatusById( )** to get current status of the subscriber. Only if it is enabled, it returns true. The **VaildateSubscriber( )** function is shown below.

```csharp
private bool ValidateSubscriber ( SubscriberHeader key )
{
    if ( key == null )
```

```csharp
            return false ;

    SubscriberTableAdapter a ;
    a = new SubscriberTableAdapter( ) ;
    try
    {
        string status ;
        status = ( string ) a.GetStatusById (
                    new System.Guid ( key.id ) ) ;

        if ( status == null )
            return false ;

        if ( status != "Enabled" )
            return false ;
    }
    catch ( FormatException fex )
    {
        // Invalid GUID format
        return false ;
    }
    return true ;
}
```

Phew! You can now heave a sigh of relief. That was one long explanation. But we hope that it was worth the trouble. After all, this is going to help you monetize your web services.

You would appreciate that to use such a web service we need to make some changes in the client code. You have two choices—either do them yourselves, or wait till the next article to where we would unravel this for you. Choice of course, is entirely yours!

Chapter 8: Nobody Is Perfect! 61

8

Nobody Is Perfect!

No matter how hard do we try, we ultimately live in an imperfect world. So though it is nice to believe that all that we have done in a web service would work correctly at all times, reality might be different. There would be so many situations where for no fault of your code an exception may occur in your web service—receiving wrong input from user, for example. There are many web services which simply return a message "failed" when such exceptions occur. Such messages are of little use. In fact, this is as good as not doing any exception handling. Ideally, an exception should be tackled in such a way that the user should get a good idea about why things went wrong.

So first we will see how to handle errors/exceptions and report them back to the client. Once we are done with that, we will show you how to create a client that uses the Subscription mechanism and incorporates error handling capabilities.

Bullet Proofing CurrencyService

Let us see what errors/exceptions we are likely to encounter during subscriber validation:

(a) Caller hasn't supplied the SOAP header.
(b) SOAP header is present but the Subscriber Id is invalid.
(c) Subscriber Id is valid but is disabled.

We can't just generate a normal exception in these scenarios. .NET Web Services use **SoapException** class to report all such errors to its clients. The details about the nature of exception are placed in a XML fragment inside a member variable in object of **SoapException** class. A sample error message may appear as shown below:

```
<ErrorInfo
    t:Message="Subscriber Key 95e62420-d529-49f4 is invalid "
    xmlns:t="http://localhost/CurrencyService"
    xmlns="http://localhost/CurrencyService" />
```

The **ValidateSubscriber( )** and **GetRateByCountry( )** methods call **getSoapError( )** method to create an exception object. This exception object is then thrown as any normal exception. This exception is reported back to the client instead or normal response to these web service APIs.

Chapter 8: Nobody Is Perfect! 63

```csharp
private void ValidateSubscriber ( SubscriberHeader key )
{
  if ( key == null )
    throw getSoapError ( "Subscriber Key is missing" ) ;

  SubscriberTableAdapter a = new SubscriberTableAdapter( ) ;

  try
  {
    string status ;
    status = ( string )a.GetStatusById ( new System.Guid
                                     ( key.id ) ) ;

    if ( status == null )
      throw getSoapError ( "Subscriber Key " + key.id +
          " is invalid " ) ;

    if ( status != "Enabled" )
      throw getSoapError ( "Subscriber Key " + key.id +
          " is not enabled" ) ;
  }
  catch ( FormatException fex )
  {
    throw getSoapError ( "Subscriber Key " + key.id +
          " is invalid " ) ;
  }
}

[WebMethod]
[SoapHeader("sHeader",Direction = SoapHeaderDirection.InOut )]
public float GetRateByCountry ( String from, String to )
{
  ValidateSubscriber ( sHeader ) ;

  try
  {
    return GetRateBySymbol ( GetCurrency ( from ).symbol,
      GetCurrency ( to ).symbol ) ;
  }
```

```
    catch ( Exception ex )
    {
       throw getSoapError ( "Invalid Country Name " +
                            ex.ToString( ) );
    }
}
```

Following function shows how the XML based error information is placed inside a **SoapException** object.

```
private SoapException getSoapError ( String message )
{
   System.Xml.XmlDocument doc = new System.Xml.XmlDocument( ) ;
   System.Xml.XmlNode node = doc.CreateNode (
         XmlNodeType.Element,
         SoapException.DetailElementName.Name,
         SoapException.DetailElementName.Namespace ) ;
   System.Xml.XmlNode details =
       doc.CreateNode ( XmlNodeType.Element, "ErrorInfo",
       "http://localhost/CurrencyService" ) ;
   XmlAttribute attr = doc.CreateAttribute ( "t", "Message",
       "http://localhost/CurrencyService" ) ;
   attr.Value = message ;
   details.Attributes.Append ( attr ) ;

   node.AppendChild ( details ) ;
   SoapException se = new SoapException ( "Fault occurred",
       SoapException.ClientFaultCode,
       Context.Request.Url.AbsoluteUri, node ) ;
   return se ;
}
```

Here we have first created a new XML document object. Then we have added a root node to this document. Name of the root node is obtained using **DetailName.Name** property in **SoapException** class. To this root node, we have added our own child

Chapter 8: Nobody Is Perfect! 65

node—**ErrorInfo** inside which, the "error message" attribute is created. Finally, **SoapException** constructor is called with three arguments:

- Source of exception ('Client' in our case. However, if it was problem with server implementation, like 'database connection failed', source should use 'Server' as the source of exception)
- The URL for which the exception occurred
- Reference to the root node.

Implementing Subscription Aware Client

Now it is time to implement the Subscription aware client. For this in the constructor **CurrencyClient( )** we have set up a subscriber id in the **service** object. This is shown below.

```
public CurrencyClient( )
{
  InitializeComponent( ) ;
  service = new CurrencyService( ) ;
  countries = new SortedDictionary<string,CountryCurrency>( );
  foreach ( CountryCurrency c in
              service.GetCountryCurrencies( ) )
    countries.Add ( c.country, c ) ;

  service.GetRateBySymbolCompleted +=
    new GetRateBySymbolCompletedEventHandler ( convComplete ) ;
  service.SubscriberHeaderValue = new SubscriberHeader( ) ;
  service.SubscriberHeaderValue.id =
          "95e62420-d529-49f4-ba79-151df61ac788" ;
}
```

When the currency conversion is completed, the client will display the time at which the conversion rate was obtained. If an exception is thrown by **CurrencyService**'s method, then the XML error report is extracted from the **SoapException** object and displayed in the client's result box. This is shown below.

```csharp
private void convComplete ( object sender,
                    GetRateBySymbolCompletedEventArgs e )
{
  ConversionPair p = ( ConversionPair ) e.UserState ;

  if ( e.Error == null )
  {
    ResultBox.Text +=
          String.Format (
          "1 {0}{1} = {2} {3}{4} ({5:dd/MM/yy hh:mm:ss})" +
          Environment.NewLine,
          p.fromC.country, p.fromC.currency, e.Result,
          p.toC.country, p.toC.currency,
          service.SubscriberHeaderValue.serverTime ) ;

    ResultBox.ScrollToCaret( ) ;
  }
  else
  {
    if ( e.Error.GetType( ) == typeof ( SoapException ) )
    {
      SoapException se = ( SoapException ) e.Error ;
      XmlDocument doc = new XmlDocument( ) ;
      doc.LoadXml ( se.Detail.InnerXml ) ;
      XmlNode n = doc.DocumentElement.Attributes.Item ( 0 ) ;

      ResultBox.Text +=
            "Failed: " + p.fromC.country + ", " +
            p.toC.country + " Error: " + n.InnerText +
          Environment.NewLine ;
    }
    else
      ResultBox.Text +=
            "Failed: " + p.fromC.country + ", " +
            p.toC.country + e.Error.ToString( ) +
          Environment.NewLine ;
  }
```

Chapter 8: Nobody Is Perfect! 67

```
  ConversionProgress.PerformStep( ) ;

  pending-- ;
  if ( pending == 0 )
  {
    ConversionProgress.Visible = false ;
    GoButton.Enabled = true ;
  }
}
```

Figures 8.1 and 8.2 illustrate the two cases—success with conversion time and failure due to invalid Subscriber Id.

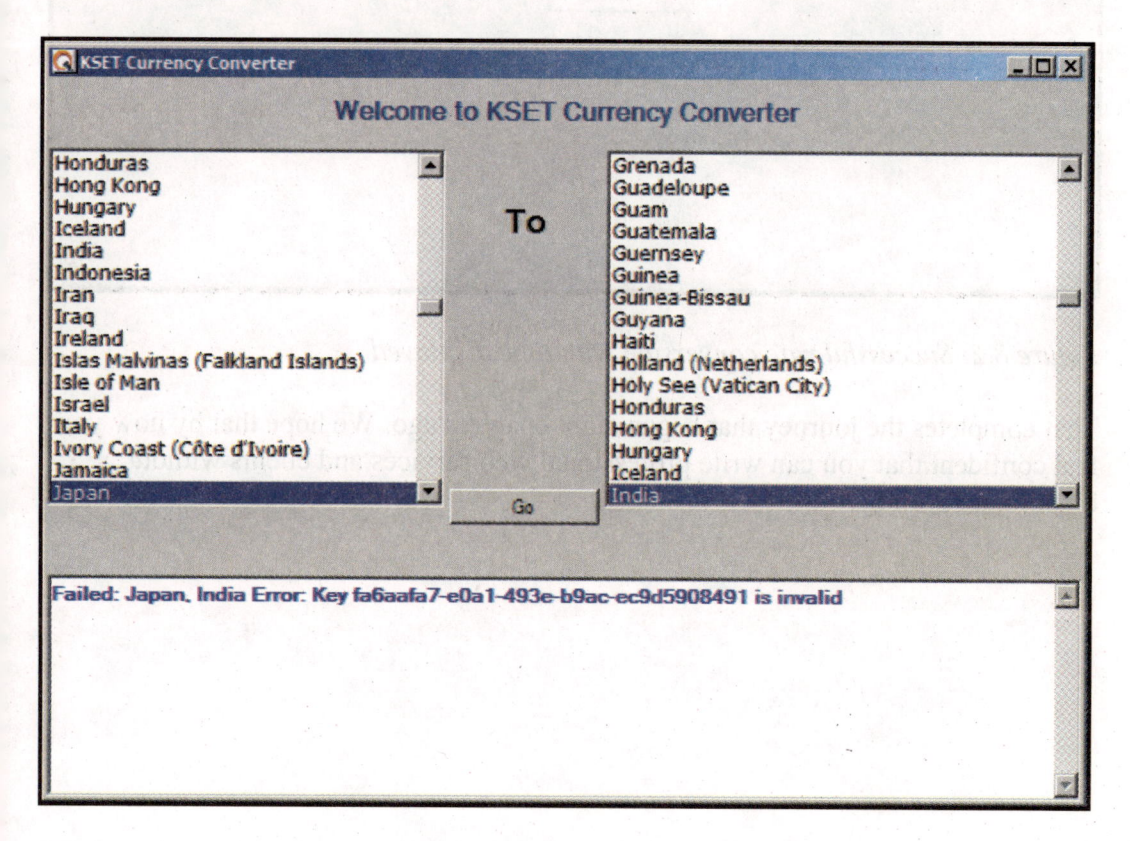

Figure 8.1: Invalid Subscriber Id

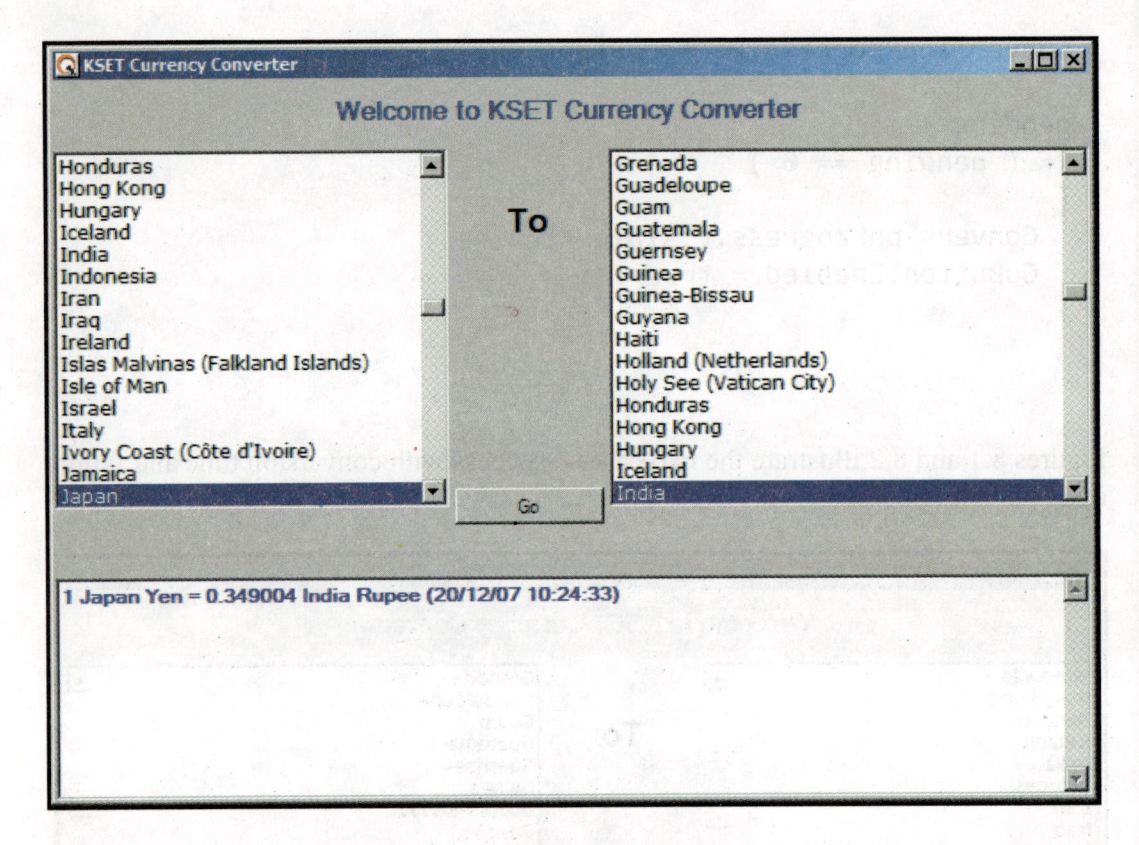

Figure 8.2: Successful rate conversion with time displayed

That completes the journey that began eight chapters ago. We hope that by now you feel confident that you can write professional web services and clients without blinking an eyelid.

Chapter 9: Until We REST! 69

9

Until We REST!

ASP.Net Web Services

Freedom to use architecture of choice has always been a dream for distributed service developers. Although SOAP based XML services have become quite popular with wide range of programmers, simplicity of standard and uniformity in implementation of these standards is certainly not the case even today. Using web services developed in .NET through Java, PHP or Javascript still remains a significant challenge. Over the years another model for creating and using web services has firmly taken roots in the realm of almost every popular web services platform today – REST. In this chapter we will show you how to modify our CurrencyService implementation to support SOAP and REST approaches simultaneously in perfectly harmonious manner.

Representational State Transfer (REST)

REST has its origins in PhD thesis submitted by Roy Fielding – one of the principal authors of HTTP specification. He proposed a new architectural style of programming in a distributed environment using an elegant and simple approach which relies on two fundamental principles:

- Represent/map the functionality of a web service using URL scheme.
- Implement the APIs using standard HTTP methods, viz: GET, POST, LIST, PUT, DELETE etc.

To make things more concrete, consider the CurrencyWebService implemented using SOAP approach. It implements following APIs:

Function	Description
CountryCurrency GetCurrency (String cname)	Returns the currency details for specified country
float GetRateByCountry (String from, String to)	Returns the latest rate of conversion from one country's currency to another
float GetRateBySymbol (String from, String to)	Returns the latest rate of conversion from one currency symbol to another
String [ ] GetCountryNames( )	Returns an array of country names

Chapter 9: Until We REST!   71

CountryCurrency [ ] GetCountryCurrencies( )	Returns an array containing names of all countries along with their currency names and symbols

Table 9.1: SOAP based Web Service Model

In SOAP based approach, WSDL is used to convey signature of APIs and associated types (e.g. **CountryCurrency**). If we follow the REST based approach, the URLs to represent corresponding APIs would be as shown in Table 9.2.

URL	Description
http://localhost/CurrencyService/country/India	GET http request on this URL will return the currency information for a country (India in our case).
http://localhost/CurrencyService/country/India/Japan	GET http request on this URL will return the latest conversion rate from Indian Rupees to Japanese Yen using country name as parameter.
http://localhost/CurrencyService/country/INR/JPY	GET http request on this URL will return conversion rate from Indian Rupees to Japanese Yen using respective currency symbols as parameters.
http://localhost/CurrencyService/country	LIST http request on this URL will return the list of country names.
http://localhost/CurrencyService/symbol/	LIST http request on this URL will return the list of countries, currency names and symbols.

Table 9.2: REST based Web Service Model

As you can clearly see, REST model captures the essence of APIs in URLs and standard HTTP operations like GET, LIST, PUT, DELETE on these URLs. This simplicity is what makes REST so appealing. While SOAP is standards based REST offers freedom to the clients of a web service. REST truly captures the essence of HTTP "resources" in URLs (or nouns) and operations (or verbs) on those resources. In the next section, we will show you how to extend the existing web service implementation to provide REST based access to **CurrencyWebService**.

REST Mechanisms In ASP.NET

To represent the APIs in a web service as URLs, we need to use a feature in ASP.NET framework to provide our own virtual paths within the web server. It would require us to parse the URL for incoming requests and map it to existing web service APIs. We will extend two abstract framework classes for this purpose:

- **CurrencyPathProvider** – extends abstract class **VirtualPathProvider**
- **CurrencyVirtualFile** – extends abstract class **VirtualFile**

By overriding **CurrencyPathProvider** will allow us to get hooked in URL parsing process and crease a "virtual" namespace of our own. **CurrencyFile** class will stream the data for a specific URL and is the heart of web service implementation. The path provider class must be registered with ASP.NET hosting environment in **Application_Start** event handler. You can add **Global.asax** file in your ASP.Net project by choosing *Add New Item* and choosing *Global Application Class*. This code is given below.

Global.asax

```
[AspNetHostingPermission (
    System.Security.Permissions.SecurityAction.Demand,
    Level = AspNetHostingPermissionLevel.High )]
void Application_Start( object sender, EventArgs e )
{
   CurrencyPathProvider provider = new CurrencyPathProvider( );
   System.Web.Hosting.HostingEnvironment
       .RegisterVirtualPathProvider ( provider ) ;
}
```

As you can notice from this code, we have created an object of our class **CurrencyPathProvider,** and registered it with the Web Hosting environment.

Let us now see the implementation of **CurrencyPathProvider**. This class should be in the **App_Code** folder of your ASP.NET web service.

Chapter 9: Until We REST! 73

```csharp
using System ;
using System.Collections ;
using System.Collections.Generic ;
using System.Security.Permissions ;
using System.Web ;
using System.Web.Caching ;
using System.Web.Hosting ;

[AspNetHostingPermission ( SecurityAction.Demand,
    Level = AspNetHostingPermissionLevel.Medium ) ]
[AspNetHostingPermission ( SecurityAction.InheritanceDemand,
    Level = AspNetHostingPermissionLevel.High ) ]
public class CurrencyPathProvider : VirtualPathProvider
{
  private CurrencyVirtualFile m_file ;
  private CurrencyService m_Service ;
  private CountryCurrency[ ] m_CountryCurrencies ;
  private List<String> m_nouns ;

  public const string cNounSymbol = "~/symbol" ;
  public const string cNounCountry = "~/country" ;

  public CurrencyPathProvider( )
  {
    m_Service = new CurrencyService( ) ;
    m_Service.sHeader = new SubscriberHeader( ) ;
    m_Service.sHeader.id ="95e62420-d529-49f4-ba79-
                           151df61ac788";
    m_CountryCurrencies = m_Service.GetCountryCurrencies( ) ;

    m_nouns = new List<string>( ) ;
    m_nouns.Add ( cNounSymbol ) ;
    m_nouns.Add ( cNounCountry ) ;
  }

  public override bool FileExists ( string virtualPath )
  {
    bool result ;
```

```csharp
   // If the path is virtual, see if the file exists.
   if ( isPathVirtual ( virtualPath ) )
   {
     // Create file and return the value of Exists property
     m_file =( CurrencyVirtualFile )GetFile ( virtualPath ) ;
     result = m_file.Exists ;
   }
   else
   {
     // if the path is not virtual, use default path provider
     result = Previous.FileExists ( virtualPath ) ;
   }

   return result ;
}

public override VirtualFile GetFile ( string virtualPath )
{
   VirtualFile file ;
   // If path is virtual, get file from virtual filesystem
   if ( isPathVirtual ( virtualPath ) )
   {
     // If file has already been created,
     // return the existing instance
     if ( m_file != null &&
          m_file.VirtualPath.StartsWith ( virtualPath,
            StringComparison.InvariantCultureIgnoreCase ) )
     {
       file = m_file ;
     }
     else
       file = new CurrencyVirtualFile ( virtualPath, this ) ;
   }
   else
   {
     // If file is not virtual, use the default path provider
     file = Previous.GetFile ( virtualPath );
   }
```

Chapter 9: Until We REST!   75

```
      return file ;
  }

  public override CacheDependency GetCacheDependency (
      string virtualPath,
      IEnumerable virtualPathDependencies,
      DateTime utcStart )
  {
    if ( isPathVirtual( virtualPath ) )
    {
      // If the path is virtual, there is no cache dependancy.
      // You could put a cache dependancy here on a file,
      // a SQL table, or some other cache trigger
      return null ;
    }
    else
    {
      // If file is not virtual, use the default path provider
      return Previous.GetCacheDependency (
          virtualPath,
          virtualPathDependencies,
          utcStart ) ;
    }
  }

  public CurrencyService Service
  {
    get
    {
      return m_Service ;
    }
  }
}

// Potential Virtual URLs
// ~/symbol/ - LIST / GET
// ~/country/ - LIST / GET
// ~/country/India - GET
// ~/symbol/INR/USD - GET
// ~/country/India/United%20States - GET
```

```csharp
private bool isPathVirtual ( string virtualPath )
{
   bool result = false ;
   string ckPath = VirtualPathUtility.ToAppRelative (
                                        virtualPath ) ;

   foreach ( string noun in m_nouns )
   {
      if ( ckPath.StartsWith ( noun,
             StringComparison.InvariantCultureIgnoreCase ) )
      {
         result = true ;
         break ;
      }
   }
   return result ;
}

public bool isValidCountry ( string n )
{
   foreach ( CountryCurrency c in m_CountryCurrencies )
      if ( string.Compare ( c.country, n, true ) == 0 )
         return true ;
   return false ;
}

public bool isValidSymbol ( string n )
{
   foreach ( CountryCurrency c in m_CountryCurrencies )
   {
      if ( string.Compare ( c.symbol, n, true ) == 0 )
         return true ;
   }
   return false ;
}

public bool isValidName ( string n )
{
   return isValidCountry ( n ) || isValidSymbol ( n ) ;
```

Chapter 9: Until We REST!   77

```csharp
    }

    public string NounRemove ( string path )
    {
        foreach ( string noun in m_nouns )
        {
            if ( path.StartsWith ( noun,
                    StringComparison.InvariantCultureIgnoreCase ) )
                return path.Replace ( noun + "/", "" ).Replace ( noun,
                        "" );
        }
        return path ;
    }

    public string NounGet ( string path )
    {
        foreach ( string noun in m_nouns )
        {
            if ( path.StartsWith ( noun,
                    StringComparison.InvariantCultureIgnoreCase ) )
                return noun ;
        }
        return null ;
    }
}
```

Let us understand this implementation one step at a time.

(a)   The constructor creates instance of **CurrencyService** class and initializes the subscriber header field. It also stores the list of currencies by invoking **GetCountryCurrencies( )** API. This will enable use to validate the virtual URL paths. Finally, it adds the "nouns" i.e. URL components that we support, viz: *country* and *symbol* in a collection of acceptable URL starting points.

(b)   **FileExists( )** is a base class function that we must override. This function has the responsibility of checking if the incoming request is a valid REST URL. It relies on private function **isPathVirtual( )** to do the real job. If the nouns are

(c) The **GetFile( )** function is another base class function that we must override. It constructs a **CurrencyVirtualFile** object for the specified virtual path and returns it to the caller. It checks if the **CurrencyVirtualFile** object already exists before calling its constructor.

(d) **GetCacheDependency( )** function returns **null** for all virtual paths that we handle. Otherwise, it uses the default path provider's implementation.

(e) Finally, we have provided numerous helper functions to extract *noun* from the virtual path, to check if the country name and symbol components are valid etc. We will show how to use of these functions, when we implement **CurrencyVirtualFile** class.

Implementing CurrencyVirtualFile

This class implements "virtual file" abstraction. This creates an illusion that the virtual path present in the URL actually exists. The data from this file object will be read by ASP.NET to generate the response. In order to generate correct response, we have to parse each virtual path to determine the web service API used and extract parameters for the request.

```
using System.IO ;
using System.Security.Permissions ;
using System.Text ;
using System.Web ;
using System.Web.Hosting ;

enum RestReqType
{
    Invalid = 0,
    ListAllCurrencies,
    ListAllCountries,
    GetCountryCurrency,
    GetRateBySymbol,
    GetRateByCountry
```

not in our list, then it invokes default provider by calling **Previous.FileExists(virtualPath)**.

Chapter 9: Until We REST! 79

```csharp
}

[AspNetHostingPermission ( SecurityAction.Demand,
    Level = AspNetHostingPermissionLevel.Minimal ) ]
[AspNetHostingPermission ( SecurityAction.InheritanceDemand,
    Level = AspNetHostingPermissionLevel.Minimal ) ]
public class CurrencyVirtualFile : VirtualFile
{
  private bool m_exists = false ;
  private string m_virtualPath ;
  private string m_Noun ;
  private string[ ] m_Parts = null ;
  private RestReqType m_reqType = RestReqType.Invalid ;
  private CurrencyPathProvider m_Provider ;

  public CurrencyVirtualFile ( string virtualPath,
        CurrencyPathProvider provider ) : base ( virtualPath )
  {
    m_Provider = provider ;
    m_virtualPath = VirtualPathUtility.ToAppRelative (
                       virtualPath.TrimEnd( '/' ) ) ;
    string cmdPath = m_Provider.NounRemove ( m_virtualPath ) ;
    if ( !string.IsNullOrEmpty( cmdPath ) )
      m_Parts = cmdPath.Split( '/' ) ;

    m_Noun = m_Provider.NounGet ( m_virtualPath ) ;
    m_exists = false ;

    string reqType = HttpContext.Current.Request.RequestType ;
    if ( m_Parts == null || m_Parts.Length == 0 )
    {
      if ( reqType == "LIST" || reqType == "GET" )
      {
        switch ( m_Noun )
        {
          case CurrencyPathProvider.cNounCountry :

            m_reqType = RestReqType.ListAllCountries ;
            m_exists = true ;
```

```csharp
                break ;

            case CurrencyPathProvider.cNounSymbol :

                m_reqType = RestReqType.ListAllCurrencies ;
                m_exits = true ;
                break ;
        }
    }
}
else if ( m_Parts.Length > 0 )
{
    if ( m_Parts.Length == 1 )
    {
        if ( reqType == "GET" &&
             m_Noun == CurrencyPathProvider.cNounCountry &&
             m_Provider.isValidCountry( m_Parts[0] ) )
        {
            m_reqType = RestReqType.GetCountryCurrency ;
            m_exists = true ;
        }
    }
    else if ( m_Parts.Length == 2 && reqType == "GET" )
    {
        switch ( m_Noun )
        {
            case CurrencyPathProvider.cNounCountry :

                if ( m_Provider.isValidCountry( m_Parts[0] ) &&
                     m_Provider.isValidCountry( m_Parts[1] ) )
                {
                    m_exists = true ;
                    m_reqType = RestReqType.GetRateByCountry ;
                }
                break ;

            case CurrencyPathProvider.cNounSymbol :

                if ( m_Provider.isValidSymbol( m_Parts[0] ) &&
```

Chapter 9: Until We REST!

```
                    m_Provider.isValidSymbol( m_Parts[1] ) )
            {
              m_exists = true ;
              m_reqType = RestReqType.GetRateBySymbol ;
            }
            break ;
          }
        }
      }
    }

    public bool Exists
    {
      get
      {
        return m_exists ;
      }
    }

    public override Stream Open( )
    {
      switch ( m_reqType )
      {
        case RestReqType.Invalid :
          break ;

        case RestReqType.GetCountryCurrency :
          return GetCountryCurrency ( m_Parts[0] ) ;

        case RestReqType.GetRateBySymbol :
          return GetRateBySymbol ( m_Parts[0], m_Parts[1] ) ;

        case RestReqType.GetRateByCountry :
          return GetRateByCountry ( m_Parts[0], m_Parts[1] ) ;

        case RestReqType.ListAllCountries :
          return ListAllCountries( ) ;

        case RestReqType.ListAllCurrencies :
```

```csharp
      return ListAllCurrencies( ) ;

    default :
      break ;
  }
  return null ;
}

private Stream ListAllCurrencies( )
{
  MemoryStream s = null ;
  CountryCurrency[ ] cc =
       m_Provider.Service.GetCountryCurrencies( ) ;
  StringBuilder sb = new StringBuilder( ) ;
  sb.Append ( "<?xml version=\"1.0\"?>" ) ;

  sb.Append ( "<Countries>" ) ;
  foreach ( CountryCurrency c in cc )
  {
    sb.Append ( "<Country>" ) ;
    sb.Append ( "<Name>" + c.country + "</Name>" ) ;
    sb.Append ( "<Currency>" + c.currency.Trim() +
                "</Currency>" ) ;
    sb.Append ( "<Symbol>" + c.symbol + "</Symbol>" ) ;
    sb.Append ( "</Country>" ) ;
  }
  sb.Append ( "</Countries>" ) ;

  s = new MemoryStream( ) ;

  byte[ ] data = Encoding.UTF8.GetBytes ( sb.ToString( ) ) ;
  s.Write ( data, 0, data.Length ) ;
  s.Position = 0 ;

  return s ;
}

private Stream ListAllCountries( )
{
```

Chapter 9: Until We REST!

```csharp
    MemoryStream s = null ;
    string[] countries = m_Provider.Service.
                            GetCountryNames( ) ;

    StringBuilder sb = new StringBuilder( ) ;
    sb.Append ( "<?xml version=\"1.0\"?>" ) ;
    sb.Append ( "<Countries>" ) ;
    foreach ( string name in countries )
    {
      sb.Append ( "<Country>" ) ;
      sb.Append ( "<Name>" + name + "</Name>" ) ;
      sb.Append ( "</Country>" ) ;
    }
    sb.Append ( "</Countries>" ) ;

    s = new MemoryStream( ) ;

    byte[ ] data = Encoding.UTF8.GetBytes( sb.ToString( ) ) ;
    s.Write( data, 0, data.Length ) ;
    s.Position = 0 ;
    return s ;
}

private Stream GetCountryCurrency( string p )
{
    MemoryStream s = null ;
    CountryCurrency c = m_Provider.Service.GetCurrency( p ) ;
    StringBuilder sb = new StringBuilder( ) ;
    sb.Append ( "<?xml version=\"1.0\"?>" ) ;
    sb.Append ( "<Country>" ) ;
    sb.Append ( "<Name>" + c.country + "</Name>" ) ;
    sb.Append ( "<Currency>" + c.currency.Trim()
                 + "</Currency>" ) ;
    sb.Append ( "<Symbol>" + c.symbol + "</Symbol>" ) ;
    sb.Append ( "</Country>" ) ;

    s = new MemoryStream( ) ;

    byte[ ] data = Encoding.UTF8.GetBytes( sb.ToString( ) ) ;
```

```csharp
      s.Write ( data, 0, data.Length ) ;
      s.Position = 0 ;
      return s ;
}

private Stream GetRateBySymbol ( string from, string to )
{
   MemoryStream s = null ;
   float rate = m_Provider.Service.GetRateBySymbol ( from,
                                                         to ) ;

   StringBuilder sb = new StringBuilder( ) ;
   sb.Append ( "<?xml version=\"1.0\"?>" ) ;
   sb.Append ( "<Rate>" + rate + "</Rate>" ) ;

   s = new MemoryStream( ) ;

   HttpContext.Current.Response.ContentType = "text/xml" ;
   byte[ ] data = Encoding.UTF8.GetBytes ( sb.ToString( ) ) ;
   s.Write ( data, 0, data.Length ) ;
   s.Position = 0 ;
   return s ;
}

private Stream GetRateByCountry ( string from, string to )
{
   MemoryStream s = null ;
   float rate = m_Provider.Service.GetRateByCountry ( from,
                                                           to ) ;

   StringBuilder sb = new StringBuilder( ) ;
   sb.Append ( "<?xml version=\"1.0\"?>" ) ;
   sb.Append ( "<Rate>" + rate + "</Rate>" ) ;

   s = new MemoryStream( ) ;

   byte[ ] data = Encoding.UTF8.GetBytes ( sb.ToString( ) ) ;
   s.Write ( data, 0, data.Length ) ;
   s.Position = 0 ;
   return s ;
}
```

Chapter 9: Until We REST!   85

}

Let us understand this implementation one step at a time.

(a) The constructor stores a reference to **CurrencyPathProvider** object. The virtual path is converted from its original form which is application relative - */CurrencyService/symbol/INR/USD* to *~/symbol/INR/USD*. This path is then split using separate / character and analyzed. HTTP Request type is found using **HttpContext** class. We only support two HTTP verbs – GET and LIST. Our request types are mapped into five operations:

- ListAllCountries
- ListAllCurrencies
- GetCountryCurrency
- GetRateBySymbol
- GetRateByCountry

The consturctor does the necessary parsing and sets **m_exists** field to true if the virtual path is found to be correct. This field is used by **CurrencyPathProvider** to determine if the virtual path exists or not.

(b) If the virtual path exists, then ASP.NET framework will use the object of **CurrencyVirtualFile** class to send the response to REST based web service client. To support this, we must override **Open( )** method in our abstract base class **VirtualFile**. The function must return a reference to a readonly **Stream** object. Depending on the virtual path, five cases arise. Each function returns a stream corresponding to five web service APIs explained above.

(c) The data format used in reponse to REST web service call is not governed by any standard. We have chosen XML as format due to its universal appeal.

(d) Private functions like **ListAllCurrencies( )** in this class simply use the existing implementation in **CurrencyService** class. The result of API call is converted into XML format and written to a **StringBuilder** object. This object is then used to construct **MemoryStream** object, reference to which is then returned to the caller. It's important to reset the **Position** in the returned stream to 0.

For every virtual path that exists, a **CurrentyVirtualFile** object is created. **Open( )** call on this object will return the XML representation of response to the client.

This completes the implementation of REST based access to our **CurrenyWebService**. As you will notice, both SOAP and REST based approaches can co-exist happily. In the next chapter, we will show you how easy it is to modify our client application to use REST instead of SOAP, so stay tuned!

10

Finally, Some REST!

Simplicity and Elegance rarely go hand-in-hand in most distributed system designs. REST is like a breath of fresh air that restores the soul of distributed programming and removes one of biggest misconceptions about HTTP – "It's a transport". It makes wonderful use of HTTP as an idiomatic protocol with nouns representing concepts (APIs) and verbs (GET, LIST, POST) representing operations. In this chapter we will show you how easy it is to write a REST client. This will convince you as to why giants like Google, Yahoo, Amazon etc. support REST in their web services.

Getting Ready to use a REST Web Service

In this chapter we will see how to modify the Currency Web Service client application explained in Chapter 2 – "Consume It Your Majesty" to use REST based approach. So as a first step, copy that project to another directory and make following changes:

(a)   Delete the Web Reference **com.ksetindia.com.ws.currency**

(b)   Remove the statement

```
using CurrencyClient01.com.ksetindia.ws.currency;
```

from **CurrencyClient.cs**.

(c)   Add a reference to **System.Web** component

With that we have removed any references to our SOAP Currency web service.

Nouns and Data Format In A REST Web Service

To develop a client for REST approach, we need to understand difference in SOAP and REST as far as API discovery is concerned. SOAP uses WSDL to describe signatures of APIs and associated data types to the client. REST unfortunately has no such support for API discovery.

The author of a web service will have to publish the URL scheme (which represents APIs), the verbs to use (GET, LIST) and response format using informal "documentation". They are auto-discovered by a client as REST doesn't force any

Chapter 10: Finally Some REST!

standard way of publishing a web service. In case of Currency Web Service, we can create a simple REST API table as shown below:

Noun	HTTP Verb	Response Format

~/country	LIST or GET	```<?xml version="1.0"?>```
		`<Countries>`
		`  <Country>`
		`    <Name>Albania</Name>`
		`  </Country>`
		`  <Country>`
		`    <Name>Algeria</Name>`
		`  </Country>`
		`</Countries>`

~/symbol	LIST or GET	```<?xml version="1.0"?>```
		`<Countries>`
		`  <Country>`
		`    <Name>Albania</Name>`
		`    <Currency>Lek</Currency>`
		`    <Symbol>ALL</Symbol>`
		`  </Country>`
		`  <Country>`
		`    <Name>Algeria</Name>`
		`    <Currency>Dinar</Currency>`
		`    <Symbol>DZD</Symbol>`
		`  </Country>`
		`</Countries>`

~/country/Name	GET	```<?xml version="1.0"?>```
		`<Country>`
		`  <Name>India</Name>`
		`  <Currency>Rupee</Currency>`
		`  <Symbol>INR</Symbol>`
		`</Country>`

~/symbol/sym1/sym2	GET	```<?xml version="1.0"?>``` `<Rate>39.9651</Rate>`
~/country/Country1/Country2	GET	```<?xml version="1.0"?>``` `<Rate>39.9651</Rate>`

This can be used to create a client for this web service. Base Address (URL) of REST web service will be augmented with nouns shown above to send correct HTTP requests to the server. Once the response is received, the client must parse the XML response and extract the data appropriately. We have created two classes to hold the result of API calls:

(a) **CountryCurrency** – Stores country name, currency name & symbol.
(b) **CurrencyRate** – Represents conversion rate between two symbols / countries.

It is important to note that we have used same class name to store currency information for each country as this class is already used in our client user interface. In SOAP based approach the class was auto-generated in WSDL import. Now, we have to implement it ourselves. The code for it is as follows:

```
public class CountryCurrency
{
  public String country
  {
    get ;
    set ;
  }

  public String currency
  {
    get ;
    set ;
  }

  public String symbol
  {
    get ;
    set ;
  }

  const string countryElement = "country" ;
  const string nameElement = "name" ;
  const string currElement = "currency" ;
  const string symbolElement = "symbol" ;
```

Chapter 10: Finally Some REST!

```
    public CountryCurrency( )
    {
    }

    public CountryCurrency ( String n, String cname,
                             String csym )
    {
      country = n ;
      currency = cname ;
      symbol = csym ;
    }

    public bool LoadFromXml ( XmlReader xr )
    {
      bool ret = false ;
      while ( xr.Read( ) )
      {
        if ( xr.NodeType == XmlNodeType.Element )
        {
          if ( xr.Name.ToLower( ) == nameElement )
          {
            country = xr.ReadString( ) ;
            ret = true ;
          }
          else if ( xr.Name.ToLower( ) == currElement )
            currency = xr.ReadString( ) ;
          else if ( xr.Name.ToLower( ) == symbolElement )
            symbol = xr.ReadString( ) ;
        }
        else if ( xr.NodeType == XmlNodeType.EndElement &&
                  xr.Name.ToLower( ) == countryElement )
          break ;
      }
      return ret ;
    }
}
```

The properties **country**, **currency** and **symbol** represent name of the country, its currency name and symbol respectively. The function **LoadFromXml( )** parses the XML fragment:

```xml
<Country>
  <Name>India</Name>
  <Currency>Rupee</Currency>
  <Symbol>INR</Symbol>
</Country>
```

The elements – Name, Currency and Symbol are parsed using **XmlReader** object and corresponding C# properties are set appropriately. If no matching XML is found or end of XML stream is reached, this function returns **false** to the caller.

Implementation of second class **CurrencyRate** is shown below.

```csharp
public class CurrencyRate
{
  public float rate
  {
    get;
    set;
  }

  const string rateElement = "rate";

  public CurrencyRate( )
  {
  }

  public bool LoadFromXml( XmlReader xr )
  {
    bool ret = false ;
    while ( xr.Read ( ) )
    {
      if ( xr.NodeType == XmlNodeType.Element )
```

Chapter 10: Finally Some REST! 93

```
      {
        if ( xr.Name.ToLower ( ) == rateElement )
        {
          rate = Convert.ToSingle(xr.ReadString ( ) ) ;
          ret = true ;
        }
      }
      else if ( xr.NodeType == XmlNodeType.EndElement &&
                xr.Name.ToLower( ) == rateElement )
        break ;
    }
    return ret ;
  }
}
```

Class **CurrencyRate** is similar in spirit. It contains a similar **LoadFromXml( )** function and it loads the object's data from XML fragment:

```
<?xml version="1.0"?>
<Rate>39.9651</Rate>
```

REST API Calls – class CurrencyRestClient

Now that we have the necessary data types to parse the response returned by REST APIs, we can implement the code to invoke the APIs. Class **CurrencyRestClient** is shown below:

```
class CurrencyRestClient
{
  private const string cGetRequest = "GET";
  private const string cListRequest = "LIST";

  private string m_BaseUrl =
        "http://localhost:4338/CurrencyService/" ;
```

```csharp
private string makeRequest ( string reqType,
    string noun, string arg1, string arg2 )
{
  StringBuilder url = new StringBuilder( ) ;
  url.Append ( m_BaseUrl + noun + "/" ) ;

  if ( arg1 != null )
  {
    url.Append ( HttpUtility.UrlEncode ( arg1 ) + "/" ) ;
  }

  if ( arg2 != null )
  {
    url.Append ( HttpUtility.UrlEncode ( arg2 ) ) ;
  }

  HttpWebRequest req ;
  req = WebRequest.Create ( url.ToString( ) ) as
        HttpWebRequest ;

  HttpWebResponse resp = req.GetResponse( ) as
                         HttpWebResponse;
  return new StreamReader (
          resp.GetResponseStream( ) ).ReadToEnd( ) ;
}

public string[ ] GetCountryNames( )
{
  String resp = makeRequest ( cGetRequest, "country",
                              null, null ) ;
  List<string> list = new List<string> ( ) ;

  XmlReader xr ;
  xr = XmlReader.Create ( new StringReader ( resp ) ) ;
  while ( true )
  {
    CountryCurrency con = new CountryCurrency( ) ;
    if ( !con.LoadFromXml ( xr ) )
      break ;
```

Chapter 10: Finally Some REST! 95

```csharp
      list.Add ( con.country ) ;
    }
    return list.ToArray( ) ;
}

public float GetRateBySymbol ( CountryCurrency fromC,
                               CountryCurrency toC )
{
    String resp = makeRequest ( cGetRequest, "symbol",
                                fromC.symbol, toC.symbol ) ;
    XmlReader xr = XmlReader.Create( new StringReader(
                                                resp ));
    CurrencyRate rate = new CurrencyRate( ) ;
    rate.LoadFromXml ( xr ) ;
    return rate.rate ;
}

internal IEnumerable<CountryCurrency>
GetCountryCurrencies( )
    {
    String resp = makeRequest ( cGetRequest, "symbol", null,
                                null ) ;
    List < CountryCurrency > list = new List <
                                    CountryCurrency >( ) ;

    XmlReader xr ;
    xr = XmlReader.Create ( new StringReader ( resp ) ) ;

    while ( true )
    {
      CountryCurrency con = new CountryCurrency( ) ;
      if ( !con.LoadFromXml ( xr ) )
        break ;
      list.Add ( con ) ;
    }

    return list ;
    }
}
```

Let us understand it one step at a time:

- **m_BaseUrl** contains the base URL of REST based web service. Before you can use the client, load the **CurrencyService** project developed in chapter 9 in Visual Studio / Visual Web Developer and launch it. Find the URL where it is deployed and substitute that address here.

- **makeRequest( )** is a helper function. It creates GET / LIST type of HTTP request with a noun and two optional parameters. For e.g., for getting conversion rate by symbol it constructs a URL

    http://localhost:4338/CurrencyService/symbol/USD/INR

    Here, the noun is **symbol**, **arg1** is USD and **arg2** is **INR**. It also takes care of encoding the URLs correctly. For example, if the country name is *United States*, the ASCII space character is not acceptable in URL. **HttpUtility.Encode( )** will convert it to *United%20States*. This function sends the HTTP request object and reads the entire response from the server. REST server's response is returned to caller of **makeRequest( )** as a string.

- **GetCountryNames( )** uses *GET* HTTP verb and noun *country* to get the list of countries in XML format. Inside this function, **XmlReader** object is created to process the list of counties and a collection of country names is filled into this collection. This collection is then returned to the caller.

- **GetCountryCurrencies( )** is almost identical except that it uses *LIST* HTTP verb with noun *symbol*.

- **GetRateBySymbol( )** uses *GET* verb with two arguments – *symbol1* and *symbol2*. It returns the conversion rate as a float.

Finally **CurrencyClient.cs** must be changed as follows:

- Replace the declaration

    ```
    private CurrencyService service ;
    ```

    with:

Chapter 10: Finally Some REST! 97

```
    private CurrencyRestClient service ;
```

- Replace the line

    ```
    service = new CurrencyService( ) ;
    ```

    with:

    ```
    service = new CurrencyRestClient( ) ;
    ```

Now we are ready to test our REST server and client. So go ahead and launch the Web Service application developed in Chapter 9 and then launch this client application. A familiar client screen will appear:

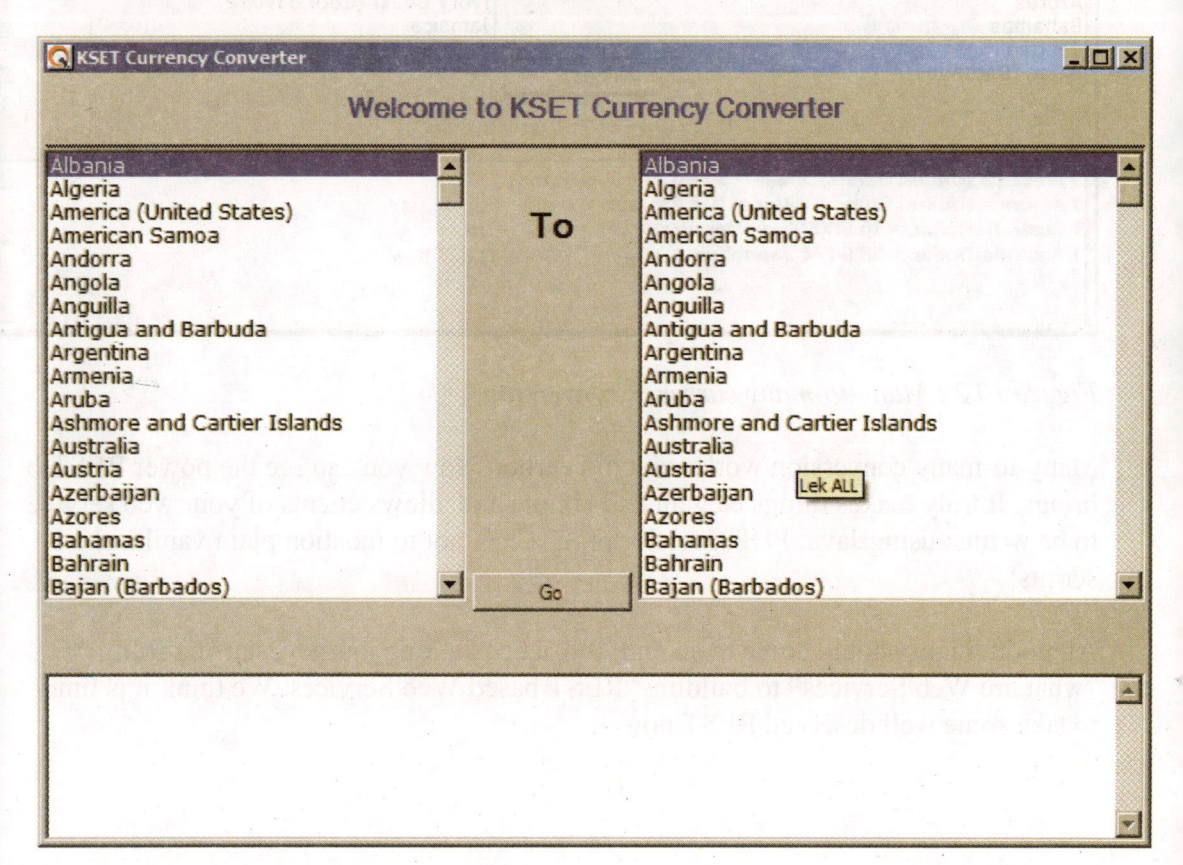

Figure 1 : Initial CurrencyClient Screen

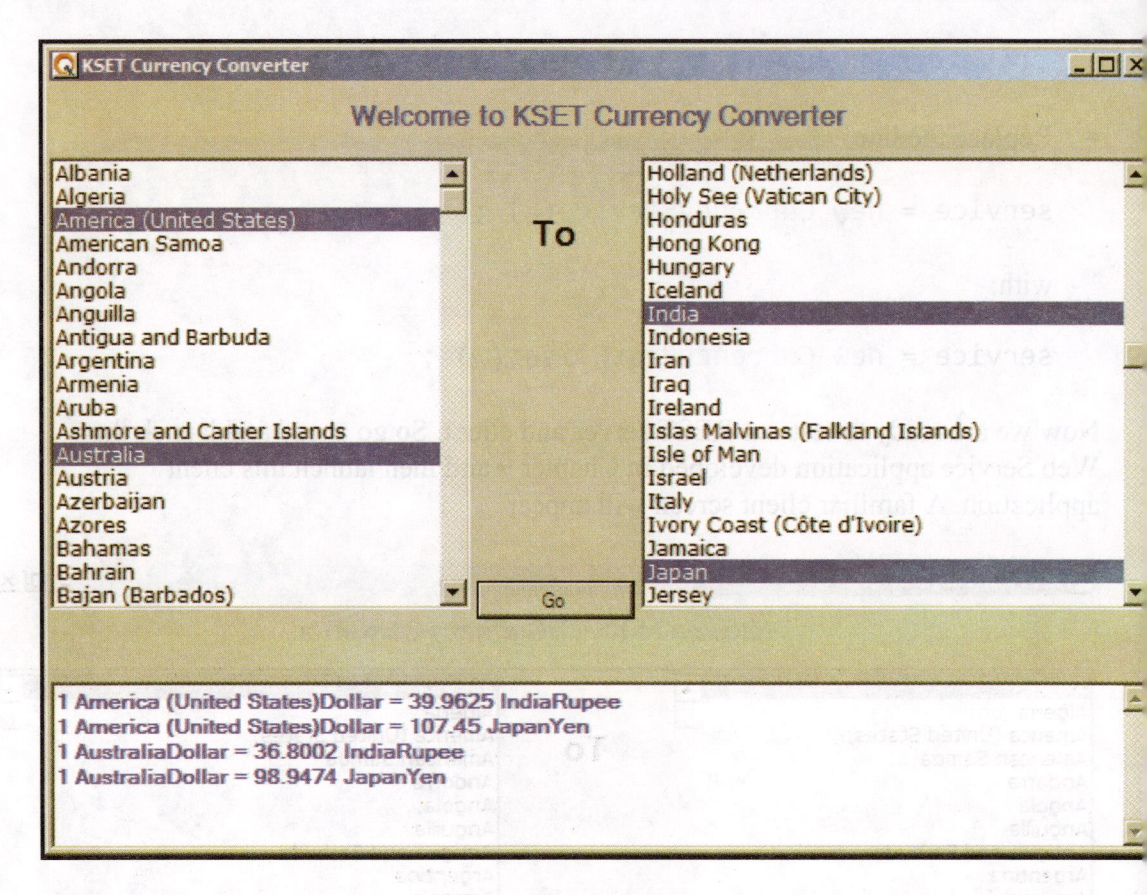

Figure 10.2 : Many-to-many currency conversion

Many-to-many conversion works as it did earlier. Now you can see the power REST brings. It truly makes things elegant and simple and allows clients of your web service to be written using Java, PHP, JavaScript, C, C++, not to mention plain vanilla shell scripts!

All good things should come to an end. It has been a long journey, starting from "what are Web Services" to building "REST based Web Services. We think it is time to take some well deserved REST now…

A

C# Primer

We have decided to use C# as the language for development of ASP.NET web services in this book. Though this book is not about C# language elements, we thought it fit to at least explain the concepts that a normal C# programmer is either not so familiar with, or is familiar with but doesn't use these concepts in everyday programming. These include concepts like generics, xml, exception handling, etc. Idea here is not to teach C# language, but to bring completeness to the book by discussing the concepts mentioned above briefly. This, we are sure would help avoid shuttling between this book and your favorite C# language book every now and then.

Again, rather than discussing these concepts in a text book like fashion, we decided to do it in a form that is a combination of slide and text. Admittedly, we are using this format for the first time. However, we believe that readers would find it useful because while developing a web service, when you are stuck up with a C# concept and wish to quickly turn to a reference that would help sort out the issue at hand, there is nothing like a slide. So what we have done is, we have taken a concept and run it through a few slides, explaining the details in the slide in a brief manner. We hope by the time you are through with this book, you too would prefer this approach.

Wishful Thinking

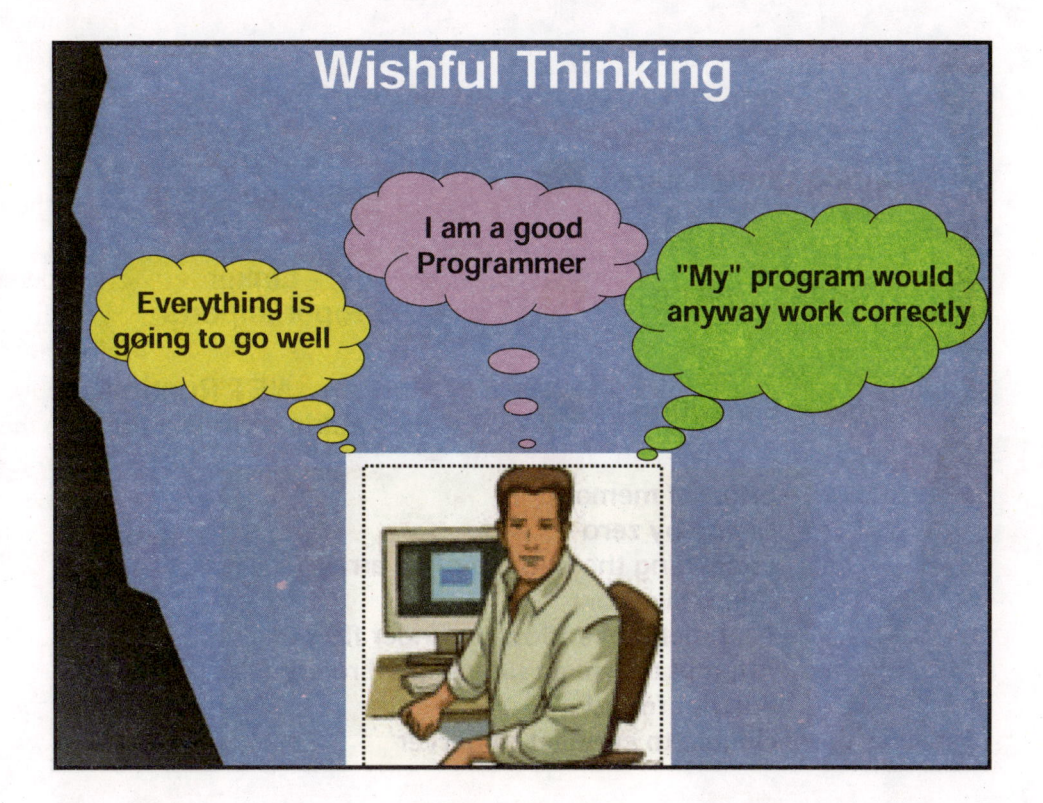

Commonly a programmer thinks that everything in his program is ultimately going to work out properly. Some also go to the extent of believing that "I am a good programmer" so what can go wrong with the program"? Or, "I have been programming for years hence I am anyway having enough skills for programming. So nothing can go wrong with my program". This however, is a false confidence. It is always good to do defensive programming rather than being over-confident about one's program.

When Things May Go Wrong

When Things May Go Wrong

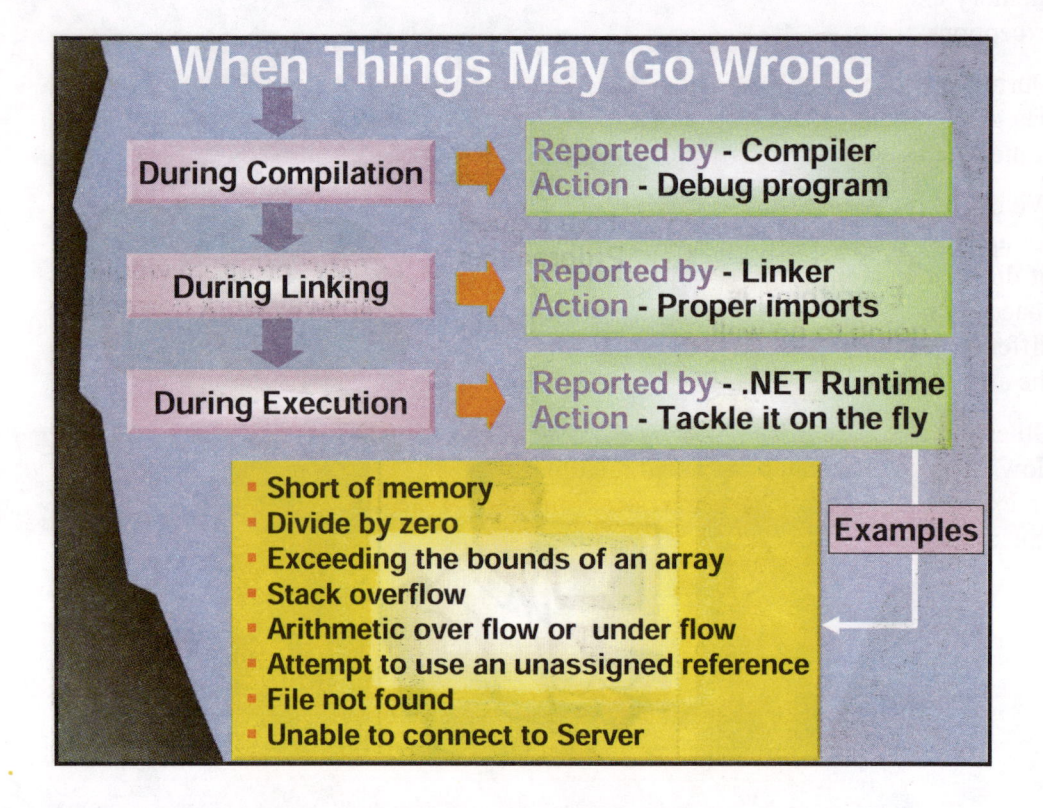

- **During Compilation** → Reported by - Compiler; Action - Debug program
- **During Linking** → Reported by - Linker; Action - Proper imports
- **During Execution** → Reported by - .NET Runtime; Action - Tackle it on the fly

Examples:
- Short of memory
- Divide by zero
- Exceeding the bounds of an array
- Stack overflow
- Arithmetic over flow or under flow
- Attempt to use an unassigned reference
- File not found
- Unable to connect to Server

When we do any program development, things may go wrong at every single stage of the development process—compilation, linking, run-time.

We first type the program and during typing itself lots of mistakes happen. We rely on the compiler to check out the grammar of the program. During compilation, if something goes wrong then the compiler assists us. Compiler tells us where these errors exist. We can rectify those errors at the compilation stage because unless and until the program is compiled correctly linking and execution cannot begin.

If during linking of the libraries with the program, something goes wrong then it will be reported by the linker and we can take care of this by writing proper imports within the program. If we do proper imports then in that case linking errors can be taken care of.

During execution if things go wrong .NET Runtime environment will report that something has gone wrong and we got to tackle that situation on the fly dynamically during execution of the program itself. Examples of things which may go wrong during execution are as follows:

Appendix A: C# Primer

We might be trying to allocate memory for an array and the memory requirement of the array is such that, that much amount of memory is not available. In that case an out of memory exception would be reported. The .NET Runtime environment would report this exception.

During execution of some arithmetic statements it might so happen that the denominator has got the value 0. If it has a value 0, the expression cannot get evaluated. In that case some exception condition will occur during execution time or runtime.

We might try to exceed the bounds of the array. Suppose we had decided to allocate space for an array by receiving the number of elements from the keyboard. We receive the value of dimension of the array in variable **n** and in code we have written statement to allocate space for **n** integers for the array and after that we may run a loop from 1 to 10 to process different elements present in the array. If **n** is supplied as 5 and we are trying to process the array 10 times then it is going to report as an error at execution time.

Other runtime exception examples include Stack overflow, arithmetic over flow or under flow, attempt to use an unassigned reference, file not found etc. All these error conditions or exceptional conditions occur at execution stage. Hence we need to tackle them at execution time.

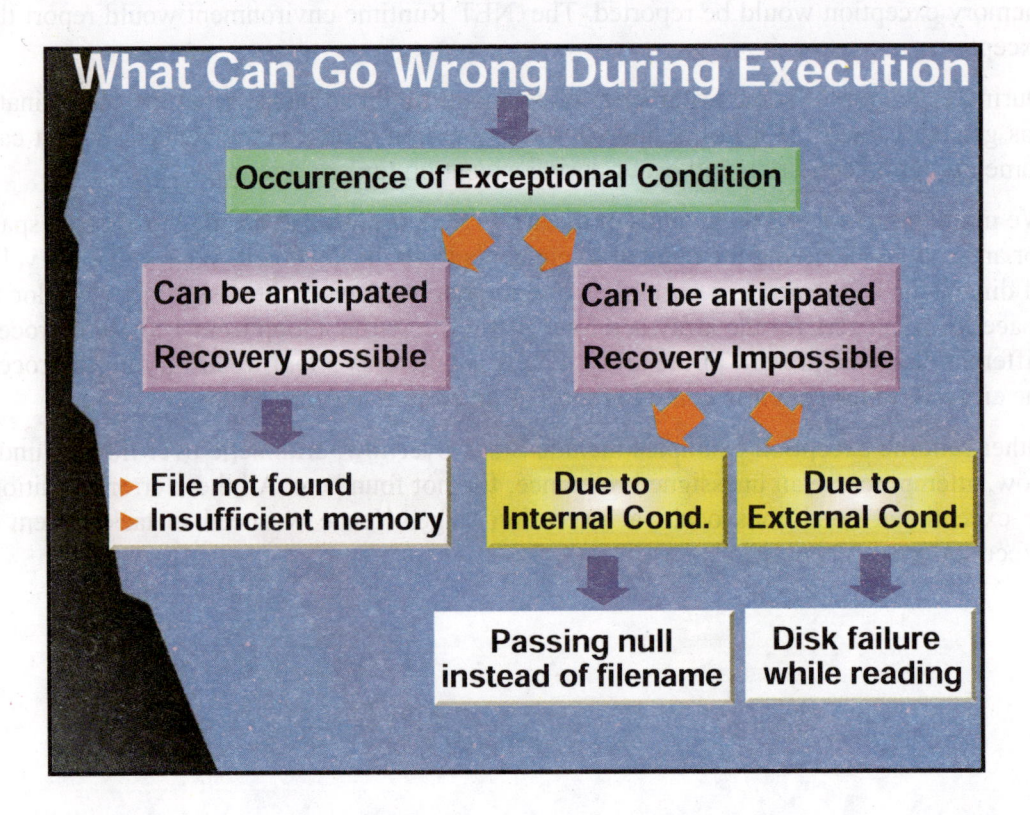

What Can Go Wrong During Execution

What Can Go Wrong During Execution

- Occurrence of Exceptional Condition
  - Can be anticipated / Recovery possible
    - File not found
    - Insufficient memory
  - Can't be anticipated / Recovery Impossible
    - Due to Internal Cond. → Passing null instead of filename
    - Due to External Cond. → Disk failure while reading

While executing a program an exceptional condition may occur. Some exceptional conditions we can anticipate and some we cannot. From those conditions that we can anticipate, recovery may be possible, whereas, from conditions that we cannot anticipate, recovery would also not be feasible. Let us understand this with the help of an example.

If we fall short of memory or if we try to open a file for reading and the file is not present on the disk then an exceptional condition can occur. Both these conditions can be anticipated and since they can be anticipated recovery from them would be feasible.

Those exceptional conditions that occur from which we cannot recover may occur due to internal conditions or due to external conditions. For example, if we are trying to pass a null instead of a file name to a function which is attempting to open a file. From this exceptional condition we cannot recover. Hence, we can say that this has occurred due to the internal condition or internal behavior of the program.

If we are trying to read the contents of the file present on the disk and as the reading was proceeding, a cyclical redundancy check error occurred. This means that the disk has

Appendix A: C# Primer

gone bad and reading from it would never be feasible. From this exceptional condition a recovery would be impossible. This is because of an exceptional condition that occurred which was beyond our imagination or control.

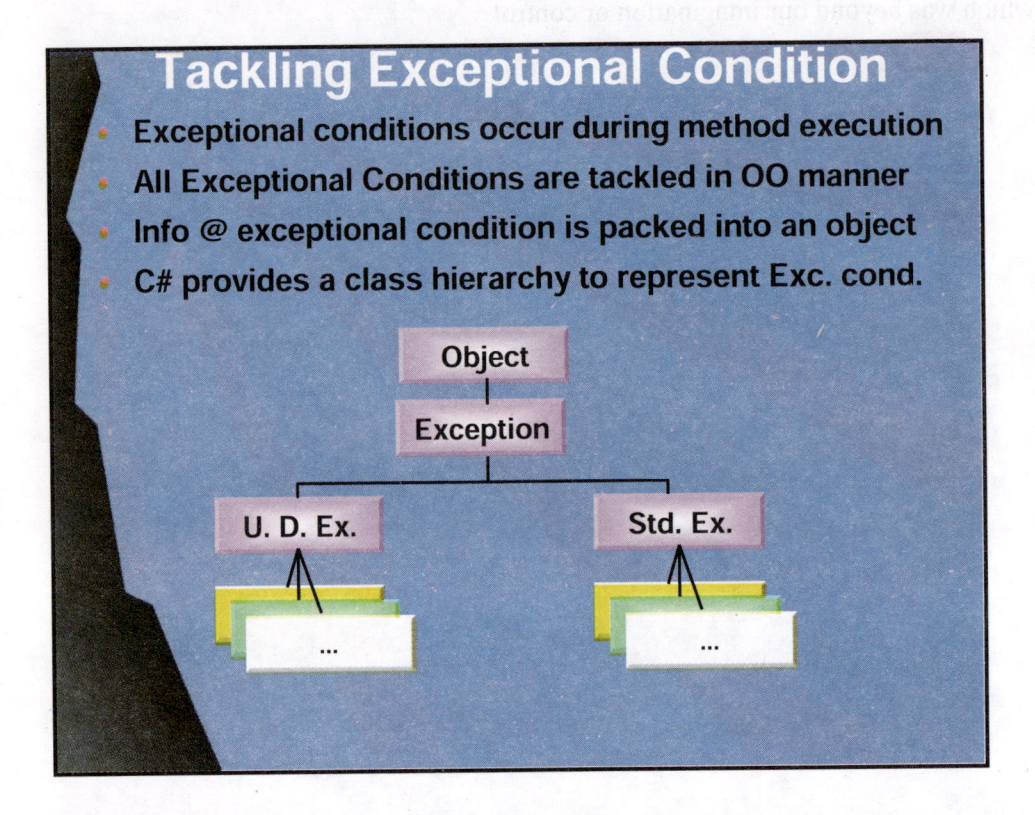

Tackling Exceptional Condition

Tackling Exceptional Condition
- Exceptional conditions occur during method execution
- All Exceptional Conditions are tackled in OO manner
- Info @ exceptional condition is packed into an object
- C# provides a class hierarchy to represent Exc. cond.

```
       Object
         |
      Exception
      /        \
  U. D. Ex.   Std. Ex.
```

Let us now understand how to tackle exceptional conditions. Exceptional conditions would occur when a method within an object is getting executed. Whenever these exceptional conditions occur, the C# model of tackling this is the Object Oriented model. Information about the exceptional condition is packed into an object and this object is thrown by the .NET Runtime Environment. If we want, we can create such an object and we can also throw it or we can leave it to the .NET Runtime Environment to gather this information into an object and throw that object. When the object is thrown, we need to catch that object and react to that exception. This is the Object Oriented way of dealing with exceptional conditions.

C# provides a class hierarchy to represent these exceptional conditions. At the top of this hierarchy, there is a class called **Object**. From the **Object** class **Exception** class is derived. There are two types of exceptions in C#; one category is known as User-Defined Exception classes and other category is known as Standard Exception classes. User-Defined Exception classes are the ones which we write. Examples of standard exception classes are **FileNotFoundException**, **InsufficientMemoryException**, etc.

Appendix A: C# Primer

Tackling Checked Exceptions

Tackling Checked Exceptions

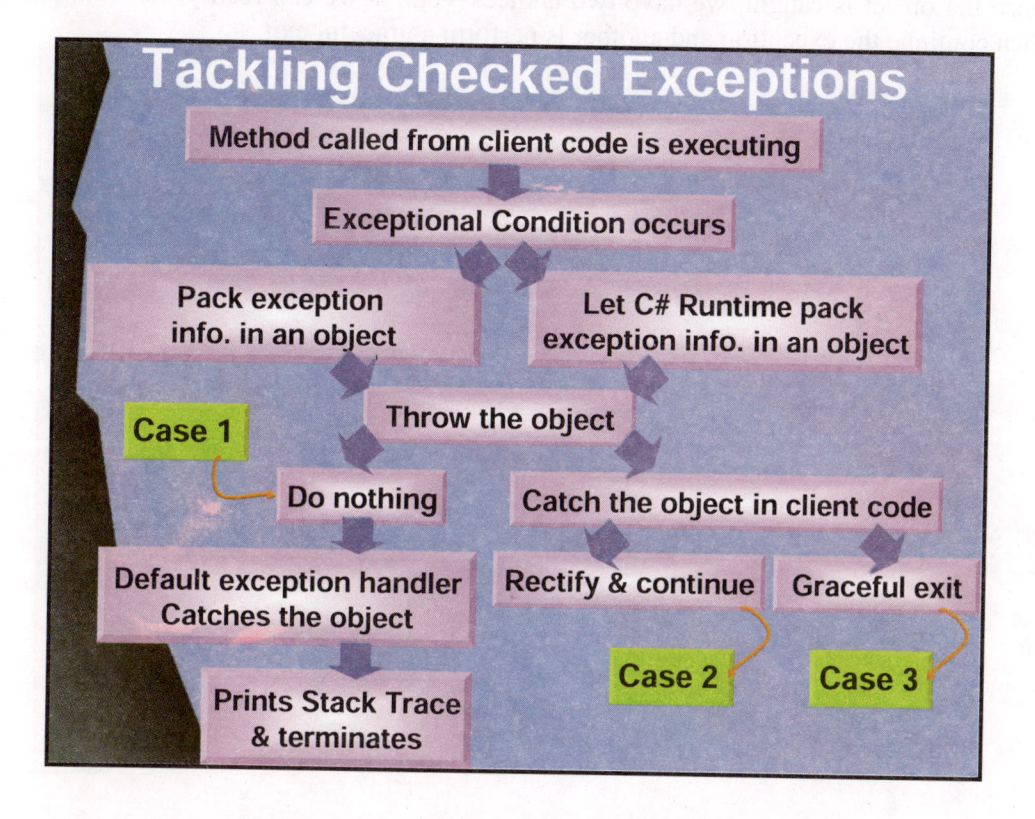

- Method called from client code is executing
- Exceptional Condition occurs
- Pack exception info. in an object / Let C# Runtime pack exception info. in an object
- Throw the object
- **Case 1:** Do nothing → Default exception handler Catches the object → Prints Stack Trace & terminates
- Catch the object in client code
  - **Case 2:** Rectify & continue
  - **Case 3:** Graceful exit

When a method is called from the client code and that method is getting executed at that time something may go wrong and an exceptional condition may occur. When this exceptional condition occurs, information about that exceptional condition would be packed into an object either by us or by C# Runtime Environment. Then that object is thrown.

Once the object is thrown, we have two choices—we may ignore the thrown object or we may catch the object in the client code. If we choose to ignore, the default exception handler that C# provides catches the object and prints out the Stack Trace and then terminates the execution. Stack Trace means the list of functions that were called before an exception occurred. For example, suppose from **Main( )** we call **fun1( )**, from **fun1( )** we call **fun2( )**, from **fun2( )** we call **fun3( )** and in **fun3( )** an exceptional condition occurs. In **fun3( )** an object will be created and thrown. If we have done nothing about this exception then the default exception handler will catch this object and then it will print out the Stack Trace. This will help us in debugging the program.

If we decide to catch the object that has been thrown either by us or by C# Runtime then once the object is caught, we have two choices—one is we can rectify the situation and then continue the execution and another is perform a graceful exit.

Appendix A: C# Primer 109

Case 1: Do Nothing

```csharp
using System ;
public class Case1
{
    public static void Main ( string[ ] args )
    {
        int i ;
        Console.Write ( "Enter a number: " ) ;
        i = Convert.ToInt32 ( Console.ReadLine() ) ;
    }
}
```

Case 1: Do Nothing

```
Unhandled Exception: System.FormatException: Input string was
not in a correct format.
   at System.Number.StringToNumber(String str, NumberStyles
options, NumberBuffer& number,
 NumberFormatInfo info, Boolean parseDecimal)
   at System.Number.ParseInt32(String s, NumberStyles style,
NumberFormatInfo info)
   at Case1.Main(String[] args)
```

- **Clumsy**
- **Bad practice**

Let us now take a look at different cases. First is the "Do Nothing" case.

In class **Case1** inside **Main( )** we wish to read a value in the variable **i** using **Console.ReadLine( )**. This program appears to be perfect. But if the user supplies a string abc instead of a number, then the integer **i** cannot hold it. So an exceptional condition would occur and since we had done nothing to anticipate this condition the .NET or C# Runtime Environment will obtain the information about the exceptional condition pack it into an object and throw it. Since we haven't caught hold of this object, the default exceptional handler will catch it and it will report an error saying that the input string that we supplied was abc, and it cannot get stored in integer **i**, so a **FormatException** has occurred.

FormatException is a class in the System namespace. The error message that has been reported by the default exception handler indicates that an exception has occurred while inputting a string in function **Main( )** of class **Case1** present in **Sample** project. Not handling an exception and just printing the Stack Trace is not an elegant way of handling exceptions.

Case 2: Recover & Cont.

```csharp
using System ;
public class Case2
{
    public static void Main ( string[ ] args )
    {
        int i ;
        while ( true )
        {
            try
            {
                Console.WriteLine ( "Enter a number: " ) ;
                i = Int32.Parse ( Console.ReadLine( ) ) ;
                break ;
            }
            catch ( FormatException e )
            {
                Console.WriteLine ( "Incorrect Input" ) ;
            }
        }
        Console.WriteLine ( "You entered: " + i ) ;
    }
}
```

Hope for the best, prepare for the worst policy

Let us now look at one more case. Here we try to receive a value in integer variable **i** in an infinite loop. We call **ReadLine( )** within a **try** block. When we anticipate things to go wrong, we should put them within the **try** block.

We receive the integer, parse that string into the integer, store it in **i** and then break outside the infinite loop. If to the **ReadLine( )** a string like "abc" is passed then it would result into an exceptional condition and when exceptional condition occurs **break** will not go to work and the exception is thrown. If the exception is thrown then we can either throw it back from **Main( )** to Runtime such that the default exception handler can tackle it or we can ourselves catch it rather than leaving it for the default exceptional handler. We catch it by writing a **catch** block. Within the parenthesis of the **catch** block, we address of the exception object (**FormatException**) thrown is assigned to **e**. After that we have displayed the message "Incorrect Input". With the infinite **while** loop, we have ensured that no matter how many times a **FormatException** occurs, we still give the user another chance to supply the correct number. When we supply the number then only the **break** within the **try** block would get executed. Outside the **while** loop, we have printed the number entered. We should try to anticipate what is likely to go wrong in the program

Appendix A: C# Primer   **111**

and then put those statements within the **try** block. Immediately after the **try** block, we have to have the **catch** block which will catch the exception that may occur. **Try** catch is a policy which says hope for the best, but prepare for the worst.

Case 3: Graceful Exit

```
using System ;
public class Case3
{
    public static void Main ( string[ ] args)
    {
        int i ;
        try
        {
            Console.WriteLine ("Enter a number: ");
            i = Int32.Parse ( Console.ReadLine( ) ) ;
            Console.WriteLine ( "You entered: " + i ) ;
        }
        catch ( FormatException e )
        {
            Console.WriteLine ( "Incorrect Input." ) ;
        }
    }
}
```

Let us now look at the third case. Inside **Main( )** in class **Case3**, we have received the integer. After receiving the number within the **try** block, we have parsed it and printed the number entered. If an exception occurs while parsing, then a **FormatException** object would be thrown. This object would be caught and an error would be reported and since we do not want to recover from it, a graceful exit would be performed.

Appendix A: C# Primer

Catching Multiple Exceptions

```csharp
Catching Multiple Exceptions
using System ;
public class MultipleExceptions
{
    public static void Main ( string[ ] args )
    {
        int i, j ;
        try
        {
            C.W ( "Enter i: " ) ;
            i = Int32.Parse ( Console.ReadLine( ) ) ;
            C.W ( "Enter j: ");
            j = Int32.Parse ( C.R( ) ) ;
            C.W ( "You entered: {0}, {1}\n", i, j ) ;
            C.W ( "Result: {0}\n", i / j ) ;
        }
```

Contd...

Let us now see how multiple exceptions can be caught. In a class **MultipleExceptions** inside **Main( )**, we have two integers **i** and **j**. Then we try to read values of these integers from the keyboard inside the **try** block because we do anticipate some error to occur while converting a string to an integer. Once the values are received we print the values of **i** and **j**. Then we would also try to print the result of **i / j**.

```
...Contd.          catch  ( FormatException ne )
                   {
                       C.W ( "Incorrect Input." ) ;
                   }
                   catch  ( ArithmeticException ae )
                   {
                       C.W ( "Arithmetic Exc. / by zero." ) ;
                   }
                   catch  ( Exception e)
                   {
                       C.W ( "Unknown Error: " + e ) ;
                   }
               }
           }
```

- **Multiple catch blocks are OK**
- **At a time only one catch block goes to work**
- **Order of catch blocks is important - Derived to Base**

Here there is a possibility of occurrence of any of the three exceptions. One is while converting **Int32.Parse( )** and attempting to store the result in **i**. This time the **FormatException** may occur or while converting the string into an integer while assigning it to **j** that time an exception may occur. Third possibility is when we try to do **i / j**, an exception may occur because **j** might turn out to be 0. If denominator is 0 then division by 0 is impossible so an exceptional condition may occur. We wish to tackle every one of these possibilities ourselves. So beyond the **try** block we say **catch (FormatException ne)** and inside it we display a message "Incorrect Input". So if value supplied to **i** is improper then also the same exception occurs and if while receiving the value of **j**, an exception occurs then that will be handled by the same **catch** block. During division if an exception occurs, it will be caught by **catch (ArithmeticException ae)**. In this case an **ArithmeticException** object is thrown, it is collect that object in **ae** and a message "Arithmetic Exc. / by zero" id displayed. Lastly we say **catch (Exception e)** where we display "Unknown Error" and the value present in **e**. Thus here we have three **catch** blocks for one **try** block.

Appendix A: C# Primer

catch (Exception e) block is written because anything other than what we are anticipating occurs that case it will be caught by the last catch block. If multiple **catch** blocks are present, at a time only one **catch** block will go to work. When an exception occurs these catch blocks will be matched one after the other. Since they are matched one after the other, the order in which we write them is extremely important i.e. we should write catch blocks from derived to base. Both **FormatException** and **ArithmeticException** classes are derived from the **Exception** class. So if we write **catch (Exception e)** as the first **catch** block then every single exception will be caught by this block. Hence we should always write the most derived exception class's **catch** block as the first **catch** block and the most base exception class's **catch** block as the last **catch** block.

116   ASP.Net Web Services

finally Block

```csharp
                            finally Block
using System.IO;
using System ;
public class Case5
{
    public static void Main ( )
    {
        StreamWriter sw = null ;
        try
        {
            sw = new StreamWriter ( "a.txt" ) ;
            sw.Write ( "Hello World\n" ) ;
        }
        catch ( IOException ie )
        {
            C.W ( "Encountered IO Error" ) ;
        }
        finally
        {
                                                          Contd...
```

Inside **class Case5** within **Main( )**, we have declared **sw** to be a reference of **StreamWriter** and set its value to null. **StreamWriter** class allows us to write to a file. Within the **try** block we have created a **StreamWriter** object through **sw = new StreamWriter ("a.txt")**. This invokes the constructor of the **StreamWriter** class and name of the file "a.txt" is passed to that. This file will get created in the current directory. Using the reference **sw**, we try to write a message "Hello World" to the file. While working with the **StreamWriter** class, if something goes wrong an **IOException** would be thrown. The **IOException** object's address is caught in reference **ie** and a message "Encountered IO Error" is displayed.

An exception may occur when we when we try to create file or when we try to write something into the file. No matter in what case the exception occurs, we want that finally some piece of code must get executed whether file writing was successful or file writing was unsuccessful. That piece of code we write in the **finally** block. **finally** is a keyword in C# specially dealing with exceptions.

Appendix A: C# Primer 117

finally Block Continued

```
...Contd.
            if ( sw != null )
            {
                sw.Close () ;
            }
        }
    }
}
```

- Code in **finally** always runs, no matter what!
  - Even if a **return** or **break** occurs first
  - Exception: Environment.Exit (1)
- Placed after **catch** blocks (if they exist)
- **try** block must have **catch** block and/or **finally** block
- **finally** clause is optional

In the **finally** block, we should try to close the file. If the file opening itself has failed then question of closing it does not arise. So we should write **finally** block taking this into consideration. We should check **if (sw != null)**. **sw** is pointing to **StreamWriter** object if the file is successfully opened. So in that case we try to close the file using **sw.Close( )**. No matter whether statements within **try** block got executed, or while executing them an exception occurred and then statements within catch block got executed, the code in the **finally** block is always going to get executed. So we usually write the clean up code in the **finally** block.

Even if a **return** or **break** occurs the **finally** block is going to get executed. Only exception to this situation is if we ourselves do **Environment.Exit (1)** and terminate the execution then execution cannot proceed further.

finally block is written immediately after the **catch** block or multiple **catch** blocks. **try** block must have **catch** block and/or **finally** block. **finally** clause is optional.

Serialization

Serialization

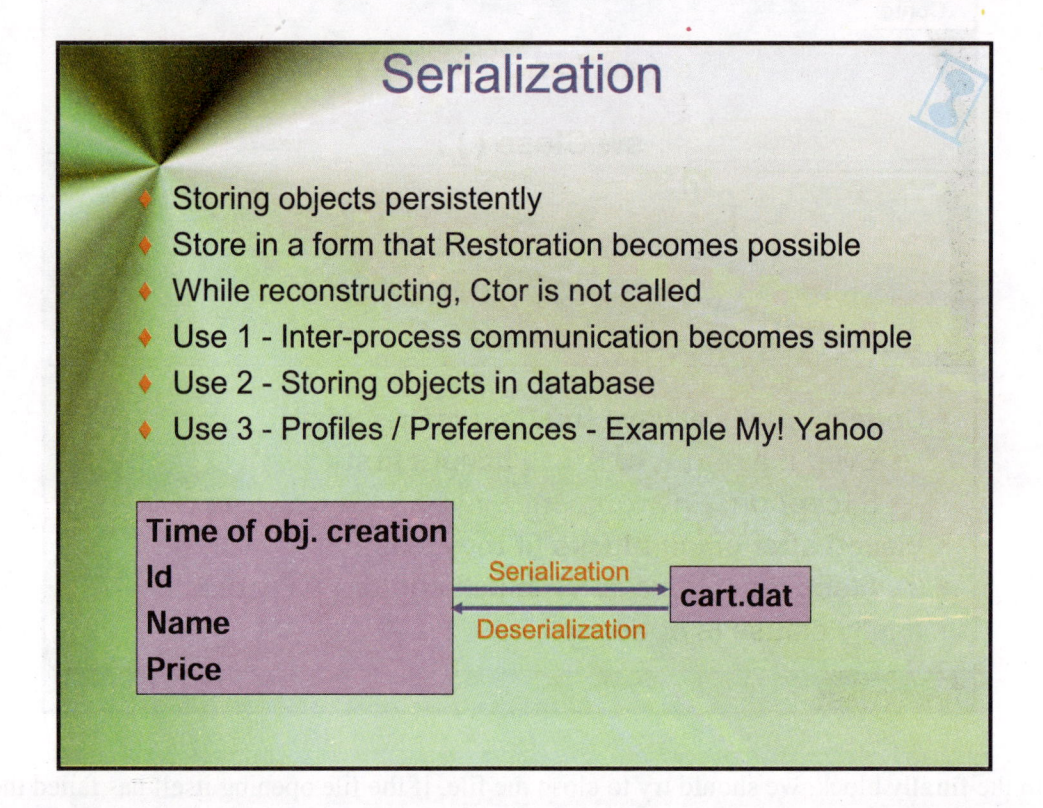

- Storing objects persistently
- Store in a form that Restoration becomes possible
- While reconstructing, Ctor is not called
- Use 1 - Inter-process communication becomes simple
- Use 2 - Storing objects in database
- Use 3 - Profiles / Preferences - Example My! Yahoo

```
Time of obj. creation
Id                         Serialization
Name                                         cart.dat
Price                     Deserialization
```

Disk is a persistent storage medium because whatever we store on the disk today is available to us to the next day. Serialization means storing objects persistently. Reconstructing the objects back is a deserialization process. We need to store the objects in such a form that restoration of objects back into memory should be feasible. When we try to reconstruct the object i.e. during deserialization, the constructor of the class does not get called.

Serialization and deserialization is useful in three cases:

- In inter-process communication

- When we want to store objects itself into a database

- For storing user preferences when we visit sites like Yahoo.com

Let us now see how to serialize an object with the help of an example. Suppose we want to serialize an object which contains four fields; time at which the object has been

Appendix A: C# Primer 119

created, id, name and the price. These four fields we want to serialize in a file called cart.dat. During deserialization we should be able to reconstruct the object.

Program

```csharp
using System ;
using System.Threading ;
using System.Runtime.Serialization ;
using System.Runtime.Serialization.Formatters.Binary ;
using System.IO ;

public class Serialization1
{
    const String filename = "cart.dat" ;
    public static void Main ( string[ ] args )
    {
        Product p1, p2 ;
        p1 = new Product ( 1, "Quest", 500.0f ) ;
        saveObject ( p1 ) ;
        Thread.Sleep ( 2000 ) ;   → Do nothing for next 2 seconds
        p2 = restoreObject () ;
        Console.WriteLine ( p1 ) ;
        Console.WriteLine ( p2 ) ;
    }
}
```

[Wed Oct 28 14:25:24 IST 2007, 1, Quest, 500.0]
[Wed Oct 28 14:25:24 IST 2007, 1, Quest, 500.0]

In this program, to begin with we import the namespaces **System**, **System.Threading**, **System.Runtime.Serialization**, **System.Runtime.Serialization.Formatters.Binary** and **System.IO**. The name of the class is **Serialization1** which contains **Main( )**. Inside the class first we have created a constant filename i.e. **const String filename = "cart.dat"**. Within **Main( )**, we have done several things related with serialization and deserialization. Inside **Main( )**, we have two references **p1** and **p2** to a class **Product**. Then we have created a **product** object by saying **p1 = new Product (1, "Quest", 500.0f)**. This object is then serialized using the saveObject( ) method. Then we have invoked a function **Sleep( )**, which is a **Thread** class method. This **Sleep( )** method postpones the execution of next instruction by 2000 milliseconds i.e. 2 seconds. Then we have restored the object by calling a method **restoreObject( )**. This method is responsible for carrying out deserialization. Once we reconstruct the object, its reference is collected in **p2**. Then we print both the objects. We have to override a method **ToString( )** within the **Product** class so that **Console.WriteLine( )** would be able to print the objects. Output of the program is shown in the slide. Last three elements in the output are same i.e. 1, Quest, 500.0. This means 1, Quest, 500.0 is present in the object referred by **p1**. It got

Appendix A: C# Primer   121

stored on the disk in a file **cart.dat**. This was done using **saveObject( )**. **restoreObject( )** restored it back. So in **p2** also we have 1, Quest, 500.0. Time also seems to have been restored. Time for 1st and 2nd objects is exactly same. But this is a problem as the 2nd object didn't get created at the time when the 1st object was created. Ideally, we should get 14:25:26 for 2nd object because we got sleep of 2 seconds for it. Hence this time for 2nd object is wrong.

Save and Restore

```
static void saveObject ( Product p )
{
    BinaryFormatter formatter = new BinaryFormatter ( ) ;
    FileStream fs = File.OpenWrite ( filename ) ;
    formatter.Serialize ( fs, p ) ;
    fs.Close ( ) ;
    Console.WriteLine ( "Serialization complete" ) ;
}
static Product restoreObject ( )
{
    BinaryFormatter formatter = new BinaryFormatter ( ) ;
    FileStream fs = File.OpenRead ( filename ) ;
    Product p = ( Product ) formatter.Deserialize ( fs ) ;
    Console.WriteLine ( "Deserialization complete" ) ;
    return p ;
}
```

Saving and restoring is done using **saveObject( )** and **restoreObject( )** methods. To **saveObject( )** we passed Product reference i.e. **p1**. We have collected it in **Product p**. Then we have created an object of **BinaryFormatter** class which is present in Serialization namespace. Then we have created a new **FileStream** object by saying **File.OpenWrite (filename)** for file **cart.dat**. Then we have called the **Serialize( )** method using **formatter.Serialize (fs, p)**. We have passed the reference of the object which is supposed to be serialized. We also need to pass the stream on which we want to write the serialized data. Then we have closed the stream using **fs.Close( )** and displayed the message that Serialization is complete.

The **restoreObject( )** method should be able to read from the file and reconstruct the object. For that it uses a **BinaryFormatter** object. We have created the **BinaryFormatter** object and then the **FileStream** object through **File.OpenRead (filename)**. This opens the file **cart.dat** in read mode. Then we have called the **Deserialize( )** method using formatter object to restore the object. Return value of

Appendix A: C# Primer   123

Deserialize( ) is a reference to the object which is being deserialized. Then we have displayed the message that Deserialization is complete and finally returned the restored object **p** which is a reference to the object of class **Product**.

Product Class

```
                                        Product Class
   Attribute – used as metadata.
   Is name of a class. More later!

[Serializable] class Product
{
    private int id ;  private String Name ;
    private float price ;  private DateTime creationTime ;
    public Product( )
    {
        creationTime = DateTime.Now ;  C.W ( " 0-arg Ctor" ) ;
    }
    public Product ( int num, String n, float p )
    {
        creationTime = DateTime.Now ;
        id = num ; Name = n ; price = p ; C.W ( "3-arg Ctor" ) ;
    }
    public override String ToString () {
        return "[ " + creationTime + ", " + id + ", " +
           Name + ", " + price + " ]";
    }
}
```

Attributes can be applied to :
- Class , Method , Member Variable
- Assembly

For the object to be serialized, we cannot write the simple class as we had done before. We have to write the class in such a way that it indicates that each object of the class is to be serialized. For that we write **[Serializable]** before the keyword **class** as shown in the slide. It is called as Attribute. **Serializable** is a class which is an attribute class. This mechanism allows us to mark the class as special. Like a class, a method, member variable and assembly can also be given an attribute. Attributes are also called metadata of a class.

Inside **Product** class, we have four private variables—**Id**, **Name**, **price** and **creationTime**. In the 0-argument constructor of the **Product** class, we have stored the current date in **creationTime** and printed a message. In the 3-argument constructor we have stored the id number, name of the product and price in three variables. In the **creationTime** we have stored the current date. Then the **ToString( )** method is called by **Console.WriteLine( )** whenever we want to print out the object. Inside this method, we have concatenated all the fields together and put them in a pair of [ ]s and returned the resultant string.

Non Seralizable Data

```csharp
Non Serializable Data

[Serializable] class Product
{
    private int id ;  private String Name ;
    private float price ;
    [NonSerialized] private DateTime creationTime ;
    public Product()
    {
        ..
    }
    public Product ( int num, String name, float p )
    {
        ..
    }
    public override String ToString( )
    {
        ..
    }
}
```

[Wed Oct 28 14:35:15 IST 2007, 1, Quest, 500.0]
[1/1/0001 12:00:00 AM, 1, Quest, 500.0]

The dates we got and the object creation time for the 1st and the 2nd object turned out to be same. But it should not have been same. If we want to avoid that then we should not serialize the **creationTime** data. For that we should declare the **creationTime** data as a non-serializable data using **[NonSerialized] private DateTime creationTime**. This declaration indicates that the date should not get serialized. The rest of the methods i.e. 0-argument constructor, 3-argument constructor and the **ToString( )** method remains same.

When we declare **creationTime** as **[NonSerialized]**, when serialization happens, only the id, name and price would get serialized. **DateTime** would not get serialized at all. For the 1st product **p1**, date would get reported correctly because **p1** has indeed been assigned the date of creation. But when we restore the object back from the **cart.dat** file since during serialization, we serialized only id, name and price; only that part of the object gets reconstructed properly. But **creationTime** is reported as different than the **creationTime** for object **p1** i.e. the default date get printed for object **p2**. So merely declaring **creationTime** as **[NonSerialized]** does not solve the problem.

Solution

```
[Serializable] class Product
{
    private int id ;  private String Name ;
    private float price ;
    [NonSerializable] private Date creationTime ;

    // 0-arg Ctor
    // 3-arg Ctor
    // ToString( ) method

    [OnDeserializing]
    void OnDeserializingMethodMethod (
        StreamingContext context )
    {
        creationTime = DateTime.Now ;
    }
}
```

[Wed Oct 28 14:34:28 IST 2007, 1, Quest, 500.0]
[Wed Oct 28 14:34:30 IST 2007, 1, Quest, 500.0]

We want that due to **Thread.Sleep( )**, the 2nd object's creation should be delayed. So in the output, we want seconds to be differing between two objects by 2 seconds. So the output we expect is 14:34:28 which is a time of creation for the 1st object and 14:34:30 as the correct time of creation of 2nd object. For this **Product** class is marked with **[Serializable]**. **creationTime** is declared as **[NonSerializable]**. 0-argument, 3-argument constructors remain same and a **ToString( )** method also remains same.

In addition to these methods, we should also provide a new method **OnDeserializingMethodMethod( )**. We assign an attribute **[OnDeserializing]** for this method. When we mark the method with **[OnDeserializing]** attribute then after all the member variables have been deserialized from the stream to which serialized or deserialized objects were returned, the serialization subsystem will provide a chance to restore the state of other variables to us. Within this method, we say **creationTime = DateTime.Now**. When we execute this program then through the output you can confirm that the object creation times would be correctly reported correctly with a difference of 2 seconds within them.

Appendix A: C# Primer

Product List Serialization

```csharp
using System ;
using System.Text ;
using System.Threading ;
using System.Runtime.Serialization ;
using System.Runtime.Serialization.Formatters.Binary ;
using System.IO ;

public class Serialization2
{
    const String fname = "cart.dat" ;
    public static void Main ( String[ ] args ) {
        ProductList pl1 = new ProductList( ) ;
        saveObjectList ( pl1 ) ;
        Thread.Sleep ( 2000 ) ;
        ProductList pl2 ;
        pl2 = restoreObjectList ( ) ;
        Console.WriteLine ( pl1 ) ;
        Console.WriteLine ( pl2 ) ;
    }
```

```
< [ 5:12:22, 0, Quest:0, 550 ][ 5:12:22, 1, Quest:1, 550 ] >
< [ 5:12:24, 0, Quest:0, 550 ][ 5:12:24, 1, Quest:1, 550 ] >
```

We can serialize and deserialize an entire collection of products. For this within **Main( )** we have created a new **ProductList** object **pl1**. Then we have called **saveObjectList (pl1)**. This indicates that entire product list is being serialized. Then the program sleeps for next 2 seconds and then restores the entire **ProductList** back by using **restoreObjectList( )**. Then we print out the entire list using **Console.WriteLine( )**. Within **ProductList** class we have to provide the **ToString( )** method. Suppose we have two products in the **ProductList**. When we execute this, they have been serialized. Their date, id, name and price have been stored. The output is shown in the slide.

Save & Restore

```
...Contd.           Save & Restore
            static void saveObjectList ( ProductList pl )
            {
                BinaryFormatter formatter = new BinaryFormatter ( ) ;
                FileStream fs = File.OpenWrite ( filename ) ;
                formatter.Serialize ( fs, pl ) ;
                fs.Close ( ) ;
                Console.WriteLine ( "Serialization complete" ) ;
            }
            static ProductList restoreObjectList ( )
            {
                BinaryFormatter formatter = new BinaryFormatter ( ) ;
                FileStream fs = File.OpenRead ( filename ) ;
                ProductList pl =
                    ( ProductList ) formatter.Deserialize ( fs ) ;
                Console.WriteLine ( "Deserialization complete" ) ;
                return pl ;
            }
        }
```

To **saveObjectList( )** we have passed **ProductList** reference i.e. **pl1**. So we collected it in **ProductList pl**. Then we have created an object of **BinaryFormatter** class and an object of **FileStream** class. Then we have called the **Serialize( )** method using **formatter.Serialize (fs, pl)**. We have passed to it the reference of the object which is supposed to be serialized. We also want to pass the stream on which we want to write the serialized data. Then we have closed the stream using **fs.Close( )** and displayed the message that Serialization is complete.

The **restoreObjectList( )** method should be able to read data from the file and reconstruct the object. For this we have created the **BinaryFormatter** object and the **FileStream** object. The **OpenRead( )** method opens the file **cart.dat** in read mode. Then we call the **Deserialize( )** method using formatter object to restore the object. Return value of **Deserialize( )** is a reference to the object that is being deserialized. Then we have displayed the message that Deserialization is complete and finally returned the restored object **pl** which is a reference to the object of class **ProductList**.

Product Class

```
[Serializable] class Product
{
    private int id ; private String Name ;  private float price ;
    [NonSerialized] private Date creationTime ;
    public Product( )
    {
        creationTime = DateTime.Now ;
    }
    public Product ( int num, String n, float p )
    {
        creationTime = DateTime.Now ;
        id = num ; Name = n ; price = p ;
    }
    public override String ToString( )
    {
        return "[ " + String.Format("{0:h:m:s}", creationTime) +
            ", " + id + ", " + Name + ", " + price + " ]" ;
    }
```
Contd...

Within the **Product** class, we have three **private** variables and a **[NonSerialized] private DateTime creationTime**. In the 0-argument constructor, we set **creationTime = DateTime.Now**. In the 3-argument constructor, id, name, price and date are set. In the **ToString( )** method, we have returned the constructed string using creationTime, id, name and price.

Product Class Contd.

Product Class Contd.

```
[OnDeserializing]
void OnDeserializingMethodMethod (
    StreamingContext context )
{
    creationTime = DateTime.Now ;
}
```

...Contd.

We have marked the **OnDeserializingMethodMethod( )** method with **[OnDeserializing]** attribute to do the reconstruction of that part of object which has been declared as **private**. For the **[NonSerialized]** data i.e. **creationTime** we will set up our new Date. Since this is called after 2 seconds, the creation time will be set 2 seconds later than the creation time that was done for the 1st and 2nd product in the product list.

ProductList Class

```csharp
using System.Text ;
[Serializable] class ProductList
{
    Product[ ] plist = new Product [ 2 ] ;
    public ProductList( )
    {
        for ( int i = 0 ; i < plist.Length ; i++ )
            plist[ i ] = new Product ( i, "Quest:" + i, 550.0f ) ;
    }
    public override String ToString( )
    {
        StringBuilder sb = new StringBuilder( ) ;
        sb.Append ( "< " ) ;
        for ( int i = 0 ; i < plist.Length ; i++ )
            sb.Append ( plist [ i ] ) ;
        sb.Append ( " >" ) ;
        return sb.ToString( ) ;
    }
}
```

The **ProductList** class is also marked with **[Serializable]** attribute. Within this class, we have two products in the **Product[ ]** array. In the constructor, we have run through a loop. **plist.Length** gives the number of elements present in that array. Each time through the loop, we have created a new **Product (i, "Quest" + i, 550.0f)**. Id **i** keeps changing for each product in the list. In the **ToString( )** method, we have created a new **StringBuilder** object, prepended that with <. Then we have walked through this array using the **for** loop. Each time through the loop, we do **sb.Append (plist[i])**. At the end, we have appended >. The resultant **StringBuilder** object is converted into string and finally that string is returned. String is immutable, whereas **StringBuilder** creates a mutable string.

Requirement

Requirement

Task:
Manage a collection of Products

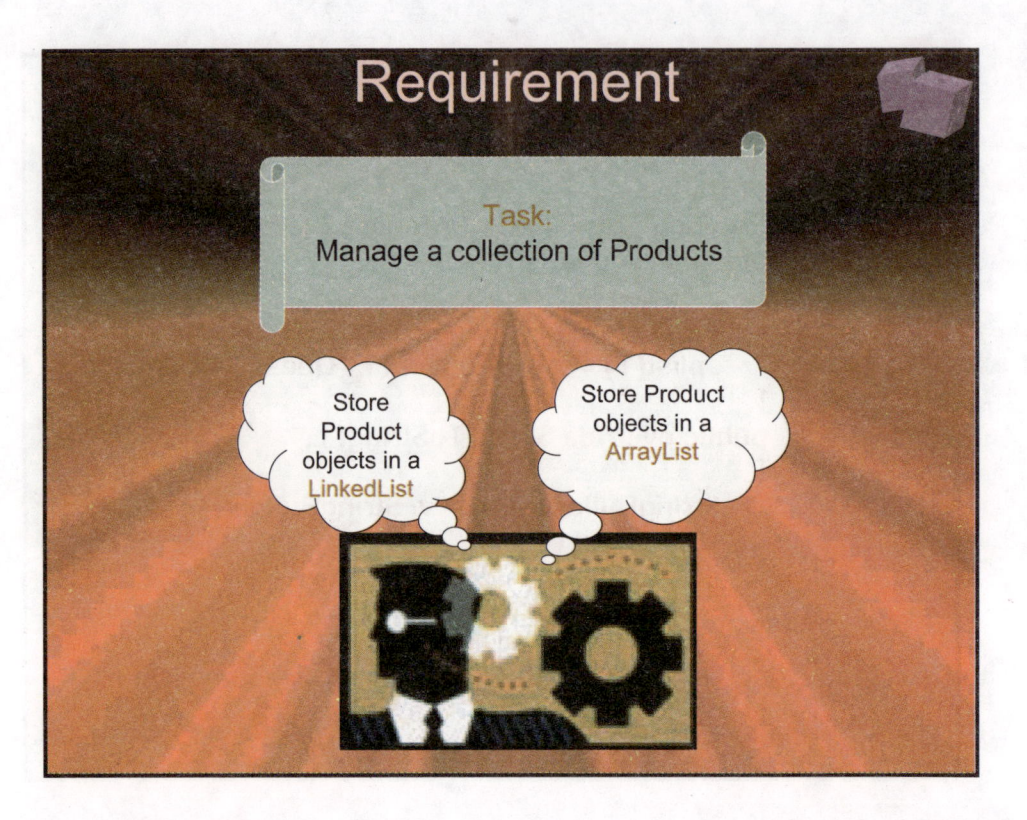

- Store Product objects in a **LinkedList**
- Store Product objects in a **ArrayList**

Suppose we have a task where we want to manage a collection of some objects of the type Product. If we want to manage such a collection then we can think of using either a LinkedList of Product objects or an ArrayList of different Product objects. We can make use of ArrayList to store collection of Products.

Product Class

```
class Product
{
    private int id ;
    private String name ;

    public Product ( int i, String n )
    {
        name = n ;
        id = i ;
    }
    public void display( )
    {
        C.W ( id + " " + name ) ;
    }
}
```

We will first create a Product class, create objects of the Product class and then store them in an ArrayList collection. We have to declare two private variables int id and String name inside the Product class. Then we have a constructor which receives an int and a String and stores them in id and name respectively. We have a display( ) function which will display the id and name on the screen.

Dump Into ArrayList

Product Class

```
class Product
{
    private int id ;
    private String name ;

    public Product ( int i, String n )
    {
        name = n ;
        id = i ;
    }
    public void display( )
    {
        C.W ( id + " " + name ) ;
    }
}
```

Now we want to build objects of the Product class and store them in an ArrayList. We import using System and using System.Collections. Name of the class is Generics1 and inside Main( ) we create an object of the ArrayList. Now we can add objects to the ArrayList using al.Add( ). We are trying to add different Product objects to the ArrayList. The id and name is passed to the constructor of the Product class. In this way we can add multiple objects in the same way. We also try to add string to the ArrayList. This is grammatically perfect. Now if we want to iterate through an array of Product objects which are present in the collection then we can use the standard way. We first call the ArrayList class's GetEnumerator( ) function. The reference is present in i. Now we can iterate through the ArrayList collection using a while loop and MoveNext( ) method. We can retrieve the objects by using i.Current. ArrayList is a heterogeneous collection which can store anything like, int, float, double, char, etc. i.e. objects of different types can go into ArrayList. ArrayList is a collection of objects and all classes in C# are derived from Object. So not only a Product object but anything primitive data can be stored in an ArrayList. Current property returns the value in the form of an Object, we have to cast it suitably i.e. Product. Its reference is stored in p. Then using p, we can call the display( )

Appendix A: C# Primer

method. For Product P1 and P2, there is not any problem. Problem will come when we try to extract string from the ArrayList because string cannot be cast into an item of the Product class. The error is an exception has occurred and name of the exception is InvalidCastException. This exception has occurred because we try to create a heterogeneous collection of Product strings unless and until we try to create an array of ArrayList objects containing only objects of the same type. Homogeneous collection is better idea than heterogeneous collection and if at all it is a heterogeneous collection then at least into that collection there must be objects which are part of an inheritance chain. The code is buggy means during compilation the code is parsed but during execution we get an exception. The code is slow because ArrayList collects only objects. It never collects the primitives. Primitives go on stack whereas objects go on heap and heap works slowly. It is ugly because it unnecessarily do the type casting.

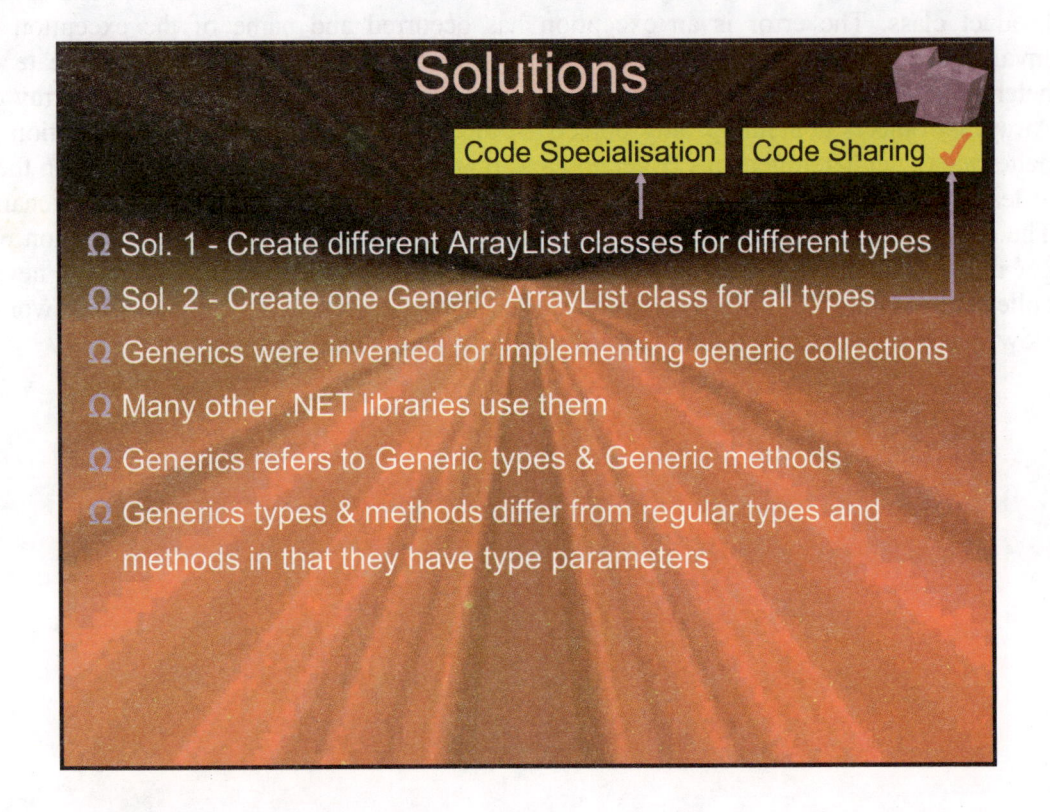

Solutions

Solutions

Code Specialisation | Code Sharing ✓

- Sol. 1 - Create different ArrayList classes for different types
- Sol. 2 - Create one Generic ArrayList class for all types
- Generics were invented for implementing generic collections
- Many other .NET libraries use them
- Generics refers to Generic types & Generic methods
- Generics types & methods differ from regular types and methods in that they have type parameters

- We can create different ArrayList classes for different types. When we use this solution means we are trying to specialize the code based on the type.

- We can create one Generic ArrayList class for all types. This is a better solution. This indicates that we share the same code no matter what the type is. This solution is implemented by generics.

- Generics were invented for implementing generic collections.

- Many other .NET libraries use them.

- Generics refer to Generic types and Generic methods.

- Generics types and methods differ from regular types and methods in that they have type parameters.

Appendix A: C# Primer

Generic List

```
using System.Collections.G     - Generic List. Other Coll. too
using System ;                 - Generic types have type parameters
public class Generics2         - Formal types replaced by actual types
{
    public static void Main ( String[ ] args )
    {
        List <Product> pl = new List <Product> ( ) ;
        pl.Add ( new Product ( 1, "P1" ) ) ;
        // pl.Add ( "hello" ) ;           - Compilation error
        pl.Add ( new Product ( 2, "P2" ) ) ;   - Ensures homogenity
                                                - Typesafe collections

        IEnumerator <Product> i = pl.GetEnumerator ( ) ;
        while ( i.MoveNext( ) ) {
            Product p = i.Current ;    - Compiles without errors
            p.display( ) ;             - No InvalidCastExceptions at runtime
        }
    }
}
```

We have a class is Generics2. Within the class we have Main( ) and inside Main( ), we say List <Product> pl = new List <Product>( ). This indicates that we are proposing to create a List of Products. Using this we invoke the constructor of the generic List class. Now we can add products to the List using pl.Add( ). When we say pl.Add ("hello"), compilation error will be displayed because we are saying that the List is a homogeneous collection of Products and we cannot add strings to that. While iterating through it, we create an iterator which works only on Products. So IEnumerator reference i is created which allows to iterate only through Product objects. Then actual iteration is carried out. i.Current return the Product object and we will collect it in p. Here no casting is required. The List class is a generic List class. Other collections are also generic. Generic collection will also have type parameters. The type parameter here is Product and it is the actual argument. When we say pl.Add ("hello"), it indicates the homogeneity and produces a type-safe collection. Typesafe means the program would compile without any errors and there will not be any InvalidCastException that will be thrown at runtime.

Generics - Tips

Generics - Tips

Ω Advantages of Generics
   Ω Increased expressive power
   Ω Improved type safety
   Ω Implicit type checks and type conversions where needed
   Ω Supports both reference and value types
   Ω Allows building generic algorithms
Ω Addition Generic features
   Ω Supports constraints
   Ω Interfaces can also be generic

- Advantages of Generics:
    - Increased expressive power
    - Improved type safety
    - Implicit type checks and type conversions where needed
    - Supports both reference and value types
    - Allows building generic algorithms
- Addition Generic features
    - Supports constraints
    - Interfaces can also be generic

Appendix A: C# Primer

User-Defined Generic

```
using System.Collections ;
using System.Collections ;
public class Generics3
{
    public static void Main ()
    {
        MyCollection <int> ti = new MyCollection <int>() ;
        ti.add ( 5 ) ;
        ti.add ( 10 ) ;
        C.W ( ti.get ( 1 ) ) ;
        C.W ( ti.get ( 0 ) ) ;

        MyCollection<Product> tp = new MyCollection<Product>() ;
        tp.add ( new Product ( 1 , "P1" ) ) ;
        tp.add ( new Product ( 1 , "P2" ) ) ;
        tp.get ( 1 ).display() ;
        tp.get ( 0 ).display() ;
```

User-Def. Generic

Output: `10 5`

Output: `1 P2` / `1 P1` — Type casting not reqd.

Within Main( ) we say MyCollection <int> ti = new MyCollection <int>( ). This indicates that MyCollection is our generic class to which int type parameter is provided. We are trying to create a collection of integer objects. Then we add integers by using ti.add( ) i.e. 5 and 10 are added to the collection. Using get( ) method of the collection, we can retrieve the values that has been added to the collection. So we get the output as 10 and 5. Then we can use MyCollection to create Product objects instead of integer objects. So the generic MyCollection can take care of integers as well as Products. We create Product collection and add Product objects by first creating Product objects and then adding them to the collection using add( ) method. We can retrieve the values from the collection using get( ) method and display( ) method. So the output obtained is 1 P2 and 1 P1. We do not make use of type casting because it is not required. The two ways ti and tp are homogenized collections. It is a concrete way of creating the collections.

MyCollection

```
class MyCollection<E>
{
    private List<E> items ;

    public MyCollection ( )
    {
        items = new List<E>( ) ;
    }
    public void add ( E obj )
    {
        items.Add ( obj ) ;
    }
    public E get ( int i )
    {
        return items [ i ] ;
    }
}
```

- E is Placeholder for any type
- E is a type parameter
- But can't assume anything
- Restrictions:
  • Can't be used in new
  • Can't be derived from

Product class:
- 2-arg Ctor
- display( )

We say class MyCollection<E>. E is the generic type. Inside class we say private List<E> items means we are trying to create items of type E. Within MyCollection constructor we say items = new List<E>( ). Means from within the MyCollection, we are trying to invoke the generic List class's collection object. add( ) method just receives the object and add it to the List using items.Add (obj). get( ) method returns something of the type E using return items[i]. We can use any other name instead of E. E is just a placeholder for a type. E is a type parameter. On the E there are several restrictions. We cannot say new E within the MyCollection constructor. It is not acceptable. From type E, we cannot derive a new type. Product class contains a 2-argument constructor and a display( ) method same as before.

Appendix A: C# Primer 141

Data Usage Scenarios

Data Usage Scenarios

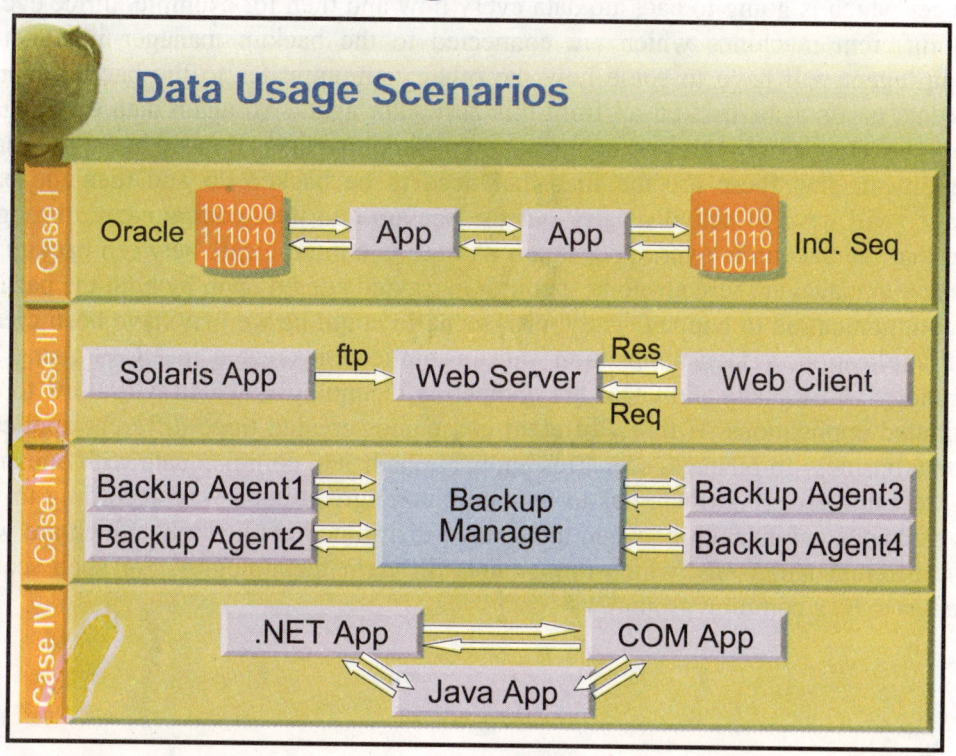

- Case I: Oracle `101000 111010 110011` ⇌ App ⇌ App ⇌ `101000 111010 110011` Ind. Seq
- Case II: Solaris App —ftp→ Web Server ⇌ (Res/Req) Web Client
- Case III: Backup Agent1, Backup Agent2 ⇌ Backup Manager ⇌ Backup Agent3, Backup Agent4
- Case IV: .NET App ⇌ COM App, Java App

The four major scenarios are as follows. One situation could be, we are using an application which is trying to read data or write data to a Oracle database. Another application might be reading data or writing data from an Indexed sequential database like a COBOL database. If these two applications who are handling data in two different ways if they want to carry out communication amongst one another then we need some common ground according to which these applications cam communicate with one another indicating that, that is how we represent a data. If one application is to send data to another, second application to send data to the first one then what is the common ground that can be used for both the applications to understand data without any confusion. This is one scenario where we need to exchange data between different applications. In another application a Solaris application using FTP uploads certain files on a Web Server. Then a Web Client that has been written either in .NET or in any such language or technology tries to send request and get response form a Web Server. This Web Server is connected to a database. How the data retrieval would happen when the Web Client makes a request and how that data would be send to the Web Client such that the client can then make use of that data. This is another scenario where the data will have to be used in such a manner that the Web Server and the Web Client agree on some ways of representing the data. Third scenario could be where we have centralized backup manager which is going to back up data every now and then for example, thrice everyday from different machines which are connected to the backup manager in a network. Backup agent will have to some how the other communicates to the backup manager. That data needs to be backed up from this particular agent. So again data exchange will have to be happen between backup agent and backup manager. Backup agent will have to communicate that these are the files that need to be backed up and then the backup manager will have to actually carry out the backup and then communicate through the agent that the backup is over. Once again its time to communicate between backup agent and backup manager there ahs to be a common ground agreed upon by both the parties for this communication to happen. The fourth scenario could be we may have been created a .NET application, a Java application and an application created in VC++ using COM technology. .NER, Java and COM are competing technologies which will allow to create distributed applications. If three different companies created three different applications and in a business-to-business scenarios applications has to communicate with one another then we can realize that there has to be a common agreed upon way according to which data exchange can happen between these three distributed applications which are written suing different languages, which implements different technologies. For such scenarios there has to be a common ground.

Appendix A: C# Primer   **143**

Moral

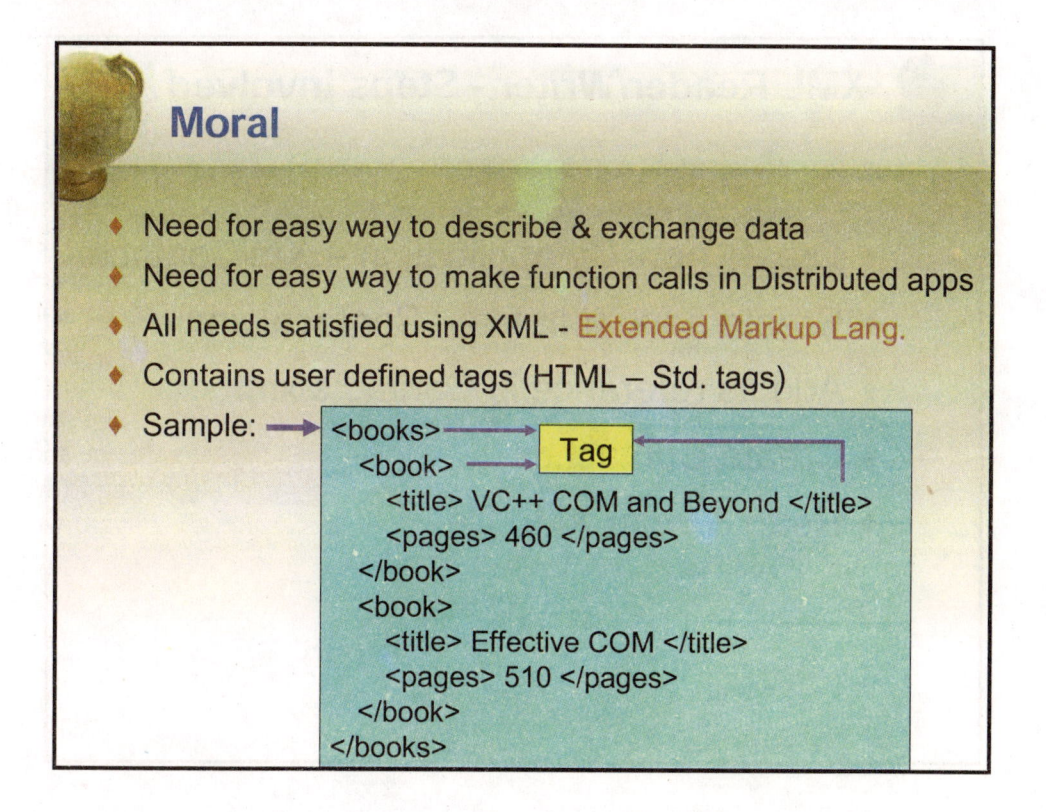

> **Moral**
>
> - Need for easy way to describe & exchange data
> - Need for easy way to make function calls in Distributed apps
> - All needs satisfied using XML - Extended Markup Lang.
> - Contains user defined tags (HTML – Std. tags)
> - Sample: →
> ```
> <books>
>     <book>              ← Tag
>         <title> VC++ COM and Beyond </title>
>         <pages> 460 </pages>
>     </book>
>     <book>
>         <title> Effective COM </title>
>         <pages> 510 </pages>
>     </book>
> </books>
> ```

- There is a need to have an easy way to describe and exchange data between two different applications.

- There is a need for an easy way to make function calls in Distributed applications.

- All needs are satisfied using XML - Extended Markup Language.

- XML contains user defined tags whereas HTML tags are Standard tags.

- The slide shows the example of XML document. The document describes a data about a book. Name of the book is VC++ COM and Beyond which has number of pages as 460. Name of another book is Effective COM and has 510 pages. books, book, title, etc. are XML tags.

XML Reader/Writer – Steps Involved

XML Reader/Writer - Steps Involved

- Create new C# application – XmlContacts
- Create new XML file – Contacts.xml
- Add its reference in Contacts.xml
- Create Contact.cs
- Read & write XML file

We want to write a XML Reader/Writer program which will read a XML document, parse it properly and based on whatever is the tag present in that document perform some action. Steps for that are as follows:

- Create new C# Application with name XmlContacts.
- Create new XML file – Contacts.xml.
- Add its reference in Contacts.xml.
- Create Contacts.cs.
- Read and write XML file.

Appendix A: C# Primer   **145**

Create Contacts.xml

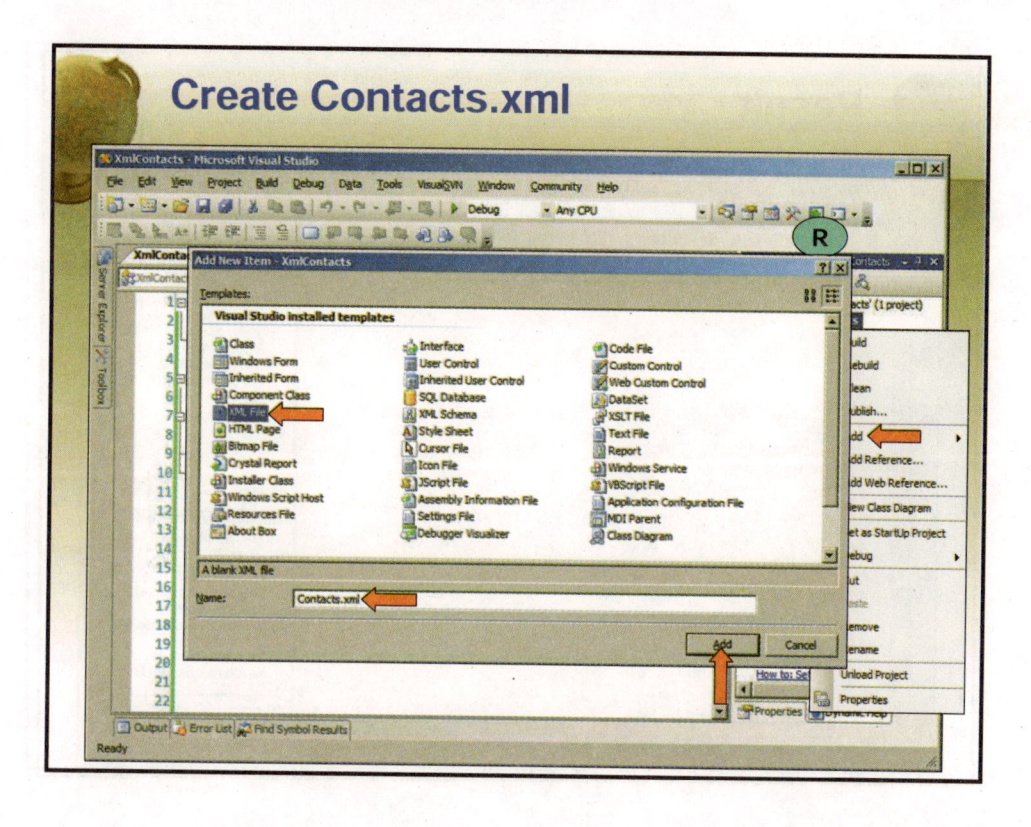

![Screenshot of Visual Studio Add New Item dialog with XML File selected and Contacts.xml entered as the name]

We have created XmlContacts project. Now we wish to add Contacts.xml file to this project. Right click on the project node, select Add. When we do so, a new dialog will appear with name Add New Item which shows kind of new item that we can add to a project. Select XML File among those entries. Provide a name Contacts.xml to the file and click on Add. So Contacts.xml will get created.

Result

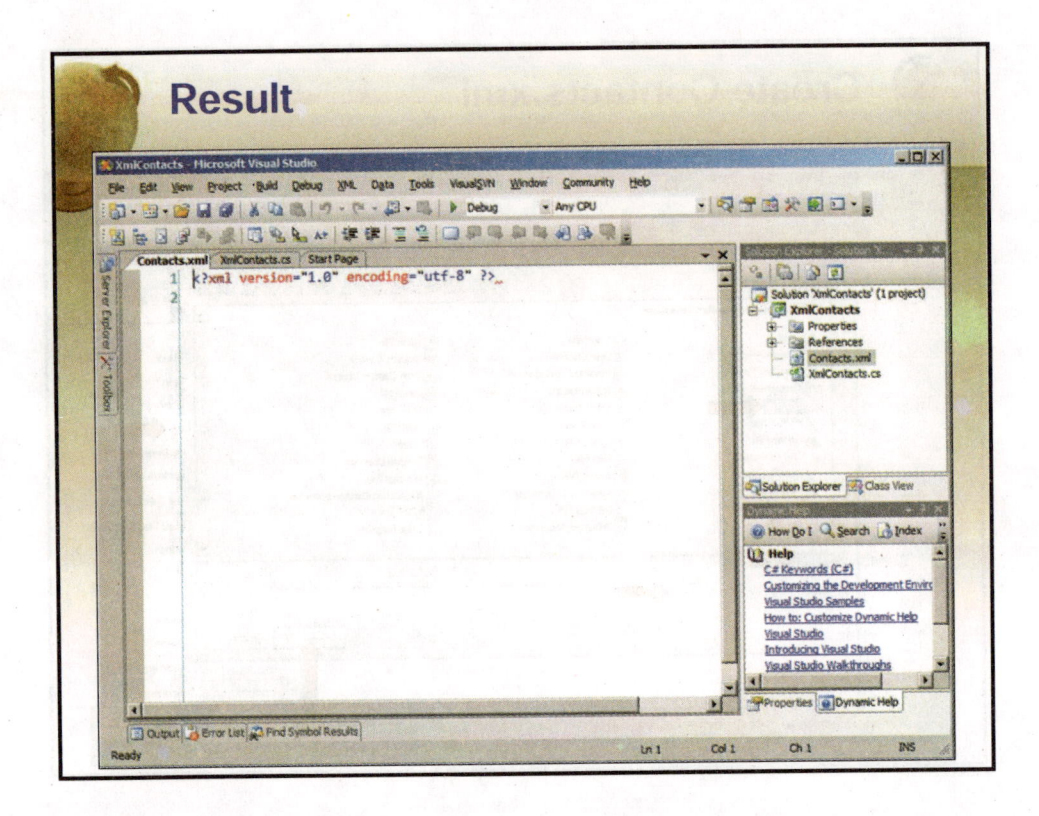

[Screenshot of Microsoft Visual Studio showing XmlContacts project with Contacts.xml file open, containing the line `<?xml version="1.0" encoding="utf-8" ?>`]

The Contacts.xml file is created as shown in the slide. Every XML document begins with the line <? xml version="1.0" encoding="utf-8" ?>. This is called as the XML declaration tag. This has to be the first line in Xml. It indicates to the parser what kind of xml document it is and what kind of encoding it uses. After that we can modify the Xml document to write the interested data.

Appendix A: C# Primer 147

Modify Contacts.xml

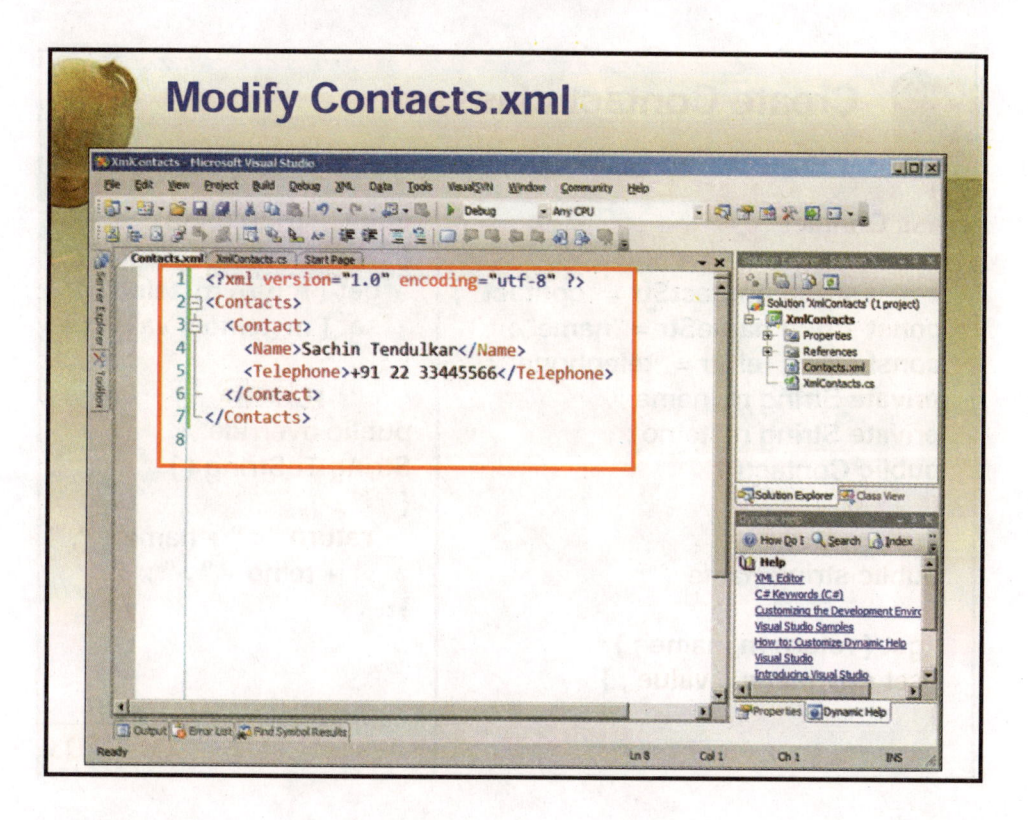

```
<?xml version="1.0" encoding="utf-8" ?>
<Contacts>
    <Contact>
        <Name>Sachin Tendulkar</Name>
        <Telephone>+91 22 33445566</Telephone>
    </Contact>
</Contacts>
```

We begin by tying the <Contacts> tag and then immediately the closing tag for that is </Contacts>. We have to maintain the level of nesting of tags correctly. Inside that we have a <Contact> tag. So for that we have corresponding </Contact> tag. Within a single Contact tag, we have Name and Telephone tags. Within Name we write name as Sachin Tendulkar whereas within the Telephone tag we have number as +91 22 45889900. Once we modified Contacts.xml, save the file.

Create Contact class

Create Contact class

```
class Contact
{
    const string contactStr = "contact" ;
    const string nameStr = "name" ;
    const string telStr = "telephone" ;
    private String m_name ;
    private String m_telno ;
    public Contact( )
    {
    }
    public string name
    {
        get { return m_name ; }
        set { m_name = value ; }
    }

    public string telno
    {
        get { return m_telno ; }
        set { m_telno = value ; }
    }

    public override
    String ToString ()
    {
        return "< " + name + ", "
            + telno + " >" ;
    }
```

CONTD..

Class name is Contact. Within the class we have private String m_name and private String m_telno. We also have const string contactStr = "contact", const string nameStr = "name" and const string telStr = "telephone". Then we provide Contact( ) zero-argument constructor which is kept as empty. Then we provide a name property. This name property is used to get and set the name. We can retrieve the name of a person using return m_name through the get accessor and we can set the name of a person using m_name = value through the set accessor. Similarly we have telno property which is used to get and set the telephone number. We can obtain the telephone number using return m_telno through the get accessor and set the telephone number using m_telno = value through the set accessor. We also provide a ToString( ) function such that if somebody tries to print a Contact object this ToString( ) function would be invoked and it would return the telephone and name written within a pair of < and >.

Appendix A: C# Primer 149

loadFromXml

CONTD..

loadFromXml

```
<Contact>
  <Name>Sachin</Name>
  <Telephone>4567890</Telephone>
</Contact>
```

```
public bool loadFromXml ( XmlReader xr )
{
    bool ret = false ;
    while ( xr.Read ( ) )
    {
        if ( xr.NodeType == XmlNodeType.Element )
        {
            if ( xr.Name.ToLower ( ) == nameStr )
            {
                m_name = xr.ReadString ( ) ;
                ret = true ;
            }
            else if ( xr.Name.ToLower ( ) == telStr )
                m_telno = xr.ReadString ( ) ;
        }
```

Reads XML file 'token' at a time

- Document
- Start Element
- End Element
- Attribute
- Text
- Xml Declaration

CONTD..

Inside the, <Contacts> tag there are multiple such blocks of <Contact></Contact>. Among them there is one such tag belong to the contact <Name> by Sachin Tendulkar. For reading from the Contacts.xml file, we have to pass a reference to an object of class XmlReader. XmlReader is a class that reads the Xml document tag by tag and then makes sure that, the tag that it is reading is of interest. For a given tag, if there is a value part, we can read that independently. For each tag is a start tag, whether its an end tag, whether it's a Xml declaration tag and so on. This function returns bool value. It returns false if the Contacts.xml that we are trying to load is not found. It returns true in case the contact is found. We are going to parse the entire Xml document. Each time we are going to create a new contact object and say for this contact object load all the properties form the Xml document. Then go to the next contact object. When the end of the Xml document is reached, this function returns false and that is the indication that the Xml document has been completely parsed. All the contacts object have been successfully created. Initialize ret = false. Then we have a while loop, that goes over xr.Read( ) where xr is a reference to the class object XmlReader. Every time we call xr.Read( ), it goes to the next token within the Xml document. Each node in the Xml document has a type. The only nodes in the Xml document that we are interested in are of type Element and of type EndElement. So we check if (xr.NodeType == XmlNodeType.Element). Other types of node are document node, attribute node, text node, declaration node, etc. Now inside that we check the name of the node using if (xr.Name.ToLower( ) == nameStr). If it is true then we say m_name = xr.ReadString( ) and ret = true. If it is not then we check if (xr.Name.ToLower( ) == telStr) and if it is true then we say m_telno = xr.ReadString( ).

Appendix A: C# Primer **151**

Slide 11

```
else if ( xr.NodeType == XmlNodeType.EndElement &&
         xr.Name.ToLower ( ) == contactStr )
    break ;
  }
  return ret ;
} // loadFromXml
```

Once again if it is not true then we check if (xr.NodeType == XmlNodeType.EndElement && xr.Name.ToLower( ) == contactStr). If this condition is true then we simply say break. Finally we return the value of ret.

writeToXml

writeToXml

```
public void writeToXml ( XmlWriter xw )
{
   xw.WriteStartElement ( contactStr ) ;
   xw.WriteStartElement ( nameStr ) ;
   xw.WriteValue ( this.name ) ;
   xw.WriteEndElement ( ) ;
   xw.WriteStartElement ( telStr ) ;
   xw.WriteValue ( this.telno ) ;
   xw.WriteEndElement ( ) ;
   xw.WriteEndElement ( ) ;
}
```

```
<Contact>
   <Name>Sachin</Name>
   <Telephone>4567890</Telephone>
</Contact>
```

We use XmlWriter class to write to the Xml document. An object of XmlWriter class is passed as an argument to the writeToXml( ) function. We begin by writing <Contact> and </Contact> tag. For every start element call we call an API xw.WriteStartElement (contactStr). contactStr contains the name of the start element. At the end of the function we have xw.WriteEndElement( ). This is so because the system maintains the order of tags that we have created and the corresponding names. For the end element it knows that whatever tag last that it was opened that is the tag closed by the end element tag. We have to put everything within these tags. We again have start element for Name. So we say, xw.WriteStartElement (nameStr). The corresponding end element for this is xw.WriteEndElement( ). So we have written the tag Name. Now its time to provide the value of the Name tag. So we say xw.WriteValue (this.name) and xw.WriteEndElement( ) to end this tag. So Name tag is completed. Now we provide the Telephone tag. So we say xw.WriteStartElement (telStr) and end this tag by saying xw.WriteValue (this.telno). In this way one contact is written in the file. For every start element, there is corresponding end element. Order of end element is important.

Appendix A: C# Primer 153

XmlTest.cs – Read/Write Contacts

XmlTest.cs – Read/Write Contacts

```csharp
class XmlTest
{
    static void Main ( string [ ] args )
    {
        List<Contact> clist = readContacts ( "../../Contacts.xml" ) ;

        Contact c = new Contact ( ) ;
        c.name = "Rahul Dravid" ;
        c.telno = "+91 22 33445566" ;
        clist.Add ( c ) ;

        writeContacts ( clist, "../../Contacts.xml" ) ;
    }
```

Class name is XmlTest inside which we have Main( ). Within Main( ), we create an object of generic List collection class clist. We are going to return list of contacts from readContacts( ) function. readContacts( ) function opens the file whose path is "../../Contacts.xml". We have a list of contacts. We can now add an extra contact to it and then write the Xml file back. For that we create an object of class Contact. Set the name of the contact as Rahul Dravid and set the telephone number as +91 22 33445566. Then using the Add( ) function in the collection class List, we added this contact object to the collection class. Then we take the collection class and pass it to writeContacts( ) function. 1st parameter is the List reference clist and 2nd parameter is the name of the file where the data has to be written. While writing we have to erase the existing and start writing from scratch.

readContacts

```
static List<Contact> readContacts ( string path )
{
    List<Contact> list = new List<Contact> ( ) ;

    XmlReader xr = XmlReader.Create ( path ) ;
    while ( true )
    {
      Contact con = new Contact ( ) ;
      if ( !con.loadFromXml ( xr ) )
        break ;
      list.Add ( con ) ;
      Console.WriteLine ( con ) ;
    }
    xr.Close ( ) ;
    return list ;
}
```

readContacts( ) function takes the path of the file, opens it and then it has to insert the objects inside the List of contacts which is a generic list. XmlReader object is created by calling a static method Create( ) in the class XmlReader. Name of the file is passed to that. It opens a file and then creates a reference to the object of class XmlReader and returns it to us. We collect it in xr and then we run an endless while loop. Inside loop, we create a new Contact object and then for that contact object we are going to call loadFromXml( ) function. loadFromXml( ) is going to load only one contact. During that processing if it finds that end of file has been reached, it returns false. So we check if (!con.loadFromXml (xr)) and if it is then we break. Otherwise that contact object which now contains the valid contact information for one contact within the file, we add to the list by saying list.Add (con). Then we display the contact on the console. Finally we close the XmlReader reference using xr.Close( ) and return list.

Appendix A: C# Primer
155

writeContacts

writeContacts

```csharp
static void writeContacts ( List<Contact> clist, string path )
{
  XmlWriterSettings settings = new XmlWriterSettings ( ) ;
  settings.Indent = true ;
  XmlWriter xw = XmlWriter.Create ( path, settings ) ;
  xw.WriteStartElement ( "contacts" ) ;
  foreach ( Contact con in clist )
    con.writeToXml ( xw ) ;
  xw.WriteEndElement ( ) ;
  xw.Close ( ) ;
}
}
```

writeContacts( ) take the List reference as the 1st argument and the file name to which the list has to be written as the 2nd argument. When we write in Xml document using the XmlWriter class, it does not indent the document correctly. So, if we open it is an editor like Notepad, it does not show it correctly. So we create an object of class XmlWriterSettings settings. Set the Indent property to true and then we say, create an XmlWriter object. To that object we pass the name of the file which has to be written and the settings that are to be used while writing the Xml document into that file. XmlWriter object is created using static Create( ) method. We begin by creating the outermost tag and its name is contacts. contacts contain multiple contact tag. So the root element in the file is contacts. So we say xw.WriteStartElement ("contacts"). Then we put corresponding xw.WriteEndElement( ). Within it, we have a foreach loop as foreach (Contact con in clist). Each time it calls con.writeToXml (xw). In this way, all the contacts are written one by one to the xml stream and in the end the tag </contacts> is written.

Test The Class

In catch block we print the name of the method and the exception message using ex.Message. Then we increment the value of failed by 1 using failed++. We can also print the current value of passed and failed. The output when we execute the program is look like as shown in the slide.